TRANSU
REAL

Transurfing

in

Days

A Practical Course
in Creating Your Own Reality

Vadim Zeland

Saint-Petersburg
Ves Publishing Group
2021

Translation by *Yoanna Dobson*

Vadim Zeland

Transurfing in 78 Days — A Practical Course in Creating Your Own Reality.

This book breaks down the Transurfing principles into 78 bight-sized chunks.

Transurfing is a powerful tool for creating your own reality. When you apply these basic principles, you will gain the power to change your destiny.

Even if you are totally new to the principles of Transurfing, you can complete the course on creating your own reality in just 78 days.

The knowledge you gain from the course, will open your eyes to the illusory nature of the external world. As you apply the principles to your everyday life, you will come to understand that physical reality does not exist as a set phenomenon in and of itself.

At each moment in time, from numerous possible decisions, you will learn how to make the one that will help you achieve your goals most effectively, and create a reality in alignment with the kinds of events that you decide do or do not have a place in your life.

Materialists focus on overcoming existing obstacles, which they tend to create themselves; idealists live in a dreamworld with their head in the clouds. Neither type is capable of shaping their own reality. With this practical course in Transurfing, you have the chance to learn how to do just that.

Subject: Esoteric / Esoteric teachings

If you don't control reality, reality will control you.

Contents

Introduction

Message to the Master

Once, in the distant past, or perhaps it was the future (it is difficult to say for certain), the Universe forgot itself. Nobody knows why. It is simply the nature of universes that from time to time, they forget themselves. She probably dozed off and could not remember her dream when she woke up. What existed before her dream? The dream before that Perhaps? Maybe the Universe WAS the dream. One way or another, the dream that could not remember itself was transformed into Nothing. Could it have been otherwise?

"Who am I?" Nothing asked itself.

"You are a Mirror... Mirror... Mirror..." Reflection responded in a gazillion flecks of light.

"Who are you?" Mirror asked.

"I am the Reflection in you."

"Where did you come from?"

"I was born of your question."

"But I cannot see you. I can't even see myself. How can I be a Mirror? I am nothing!"

"Exactly," Reflection answered. "Emptiness is, in essence, the most primordial and infinitely multi-dimensional mirror of all because, in the void, nothing reflects nothing."

"What do I look like?"

"You don't look like anything."

"Am I big or small?"

"Yes."

"What do you mean, yes?"

"You are both. You are as you imagine yourself to be. You are both infinitely big and infinitely small at the same time because infinity and a dot are the same thing."

"How strange. So, where am I?"

"Right now, you are in the variants space," Reflection answered.

"Variants of what?"

"Anything at all. The space also appeared as a result of your question. Everything you think about comes into being, for you are an infinitely multi-dimensional Mirror. To your every question there exists an infinite number of answers."

"Why do I exist?"

"To be."

"What can I do?"

"Anything."

The world was created in the dialogue between the Mirror, which we call God, and Reflection. Welcome, dear Master. I am writing you this message because you are reading these lines, which means you intend to become the ruler of your own world and destiny.

In ancient times, everyone was a master in as much as they knew that there are two sides to reality: one physical, the other metaphysical. The masters saw and understood the nature of the mirror world. They knew how to create their own reality with the power of thought. Things did not stay that way for long though. With time, the masters' attention became locked in material reality. They stopped being able to see and unlearned their power. Nonetheless, their knowledge was not lost. From the depths of time, it survived over millennia to the present day.

The sorcerers of antiquity, the knowledge carriers, were able to control reality by the power of thought because reality is primarily created as a reflection of consciousness in the Mirror of the world. Those whose consciousness is limited to a material worldview have to make do with worshipping contrived gods and turning to the services of astrologers and fortune-tellers.

If you don't want to settle for a surrogate future, at which a fortune-teller claims they can take a sneak peek, if you intend to master your destiny according to your own will, you will certainly succeed. Transurfing, universal knowledge of how to shape reality, is designed to help you.

There is no magic to Transurfing. Magic, as such, does not exist. It is really just knowledge of the principles of the Mirror world. The knowledge itself is fairly self-explanatory. In fact, it is so simple and commonplace that it could not count as 'magic' by any stretch of the imagination. And still, Aladdin's Lamp looked like it was just a bit of old tin and the Holy Grail was not made of gold. Everything truly great is unfathomably simple and has no need to show off or hide. In contrast, things that are superficial and of no real worth tend to be masked under a veil of magnificence and mystery.

When magic is stripped of its fairy tale attributes and embedded in daily life, it ceases to belong to the realm of the mystical and the unexplained. It loses its fascinating mystique because it is bang in the middle of everyday life. The beauty of the transformation is that everyday life no longer seems dull and ordinary. It transforms into a new reality that can be shaped as long as you follow certain rules.

This book outlines the set of basic principles essential to creating your own reality. The Transurfing principles fall into two basic categories relating to thoughts and actions. When these categories reflect in the dual mirror of our world, they give rise to their opposites. So, on either side of the dual mirror there are Reason (logic) and Soul (heart), Action (inner intention) and Passivity (outer intention).

The motivation, thoughts and actions of the subject being reflected have to be in balance with these four elements. Reason and Action relate to the physical world; Soul and Passivity relate to the metaphysical world, which is a reality no less objective than its material counterpart. If you only take one facet of the dual world into account, you will never succeed in shaping your own reality. This is why materialists busy themselves overcoming obstacles, which they have basically created themselves and idealists float about in a world of clouds and dreams. Neither can successfully shape their reality.

But you can learn how to.

Even if you are unfamiliar with the principles of Transurfing, you can complete this practical course in creating your own reality within 78 days. Each morning, read one principle and its interpretation and try to implement it throughout the rest of the day. The next day, move on to the next principle, remembering to practice the principles you have covered previously.

Continue in this way until you have assimilated all the principles consecutively. Of course, this is a relatively extended process but it is the most effective way of assimilating the principles. Creating your own reality mostly comes down to practice.

In applying the principles, listen to your intuition and trust your intuition. Good Luck!

Reality in an unfamiliar guise

Since time immemorial, people have understood that the world behaves in a dual manner. On the one hand, everything that happens on the material level is more or less clear and can be explained from the point of view of the laws of natural science. On the other hand, when we encounter phenomena originating in the subtle planes, these laws are no longer applicable. Why has not it ever been possible to unite different manifestations of reality into a single knowledge system?

Strangely, it is as if the world were playing hide-and-seek with us, not wanting to reveal its true essence. As soon as scientists discover a new law to explain one phenomenon, another appears to contradict it. This pursuit of truth is as elusive as a shadow and will go on forever. The interesting thing is that the world does not just hide its true face; it willingly takes on whatever guise we attribute to it.

This is clearly evident in all branches of science. For example, if you imagine that a microcosm consists of particles then there will be no shortage of experiments to support this supposition. If you assume that the microcosm is not a particle but an electromagnetic wave, the world won't object, and will readily manifest itself accordingly.

You could ask the world whether it consisted of solid matter with just the same success. It would answer 'yes'. Or maybe it consists of energy? Again, it will answer in the affirmative. As we know, micro-particles in a vacuum are constantly being created and annihilated as energy is transformed into matter, and vice versa.

It would be futile to ask the world what came first, matter or consciousness. It would change its mask just as cunningly, revealing to us whatever side of the world we wished to see. Representatives of various teachings argue with each other, each trying to prove an opposing point of view, but reality will always pass a dispassionate verdict because, in essence, they are all right.

The world agrees with us and dodges us at the same time. In other words, it acts like a mirror. It literally reflects all of our notions of reality, whatever they happen to be.

So where does that leave us? If the world always agrees with what we think about it, at the same time, constantly evading a direct answer, are not all our attempts to explain the nature of reality in vain?

The fact is everything is much simpler than that. There is no point in searching for an absolute truth in individual manifestations of a multifaceted reality. We just have to accept the fact that reality as a mirror has two aspects. A physical aspect, which you can touch, and a metaphysical aspect, which lies beyond the limits of perception and yet is no less objective in nature.

At the present time, science deals with the side of life that is reflected in the mirror, whereas esotericism tries to look at life outside the mirror. The entire debate basically boils down to a difference in focus. So what exactly does lie on the other side of the mirror?

Transurfing, like any esoteric teaching, offers one of many possible answers to this question. On the other side of the mirror glass there lies the 'variants space,' an information structure, that stores the scripts to all possible events. The number of variants is infinite, as infinite as the number of possible positions of a single dot on a grid. The variants space is a record of everything that ever was and everything that will ever be.

This also means that access to the variants space provides the opportunity for clairvoyance. The only setback is that because the number of variants is infinite, one can see events that will not be realised in physical reality. This is why clairvoyants often make 'mistakes' in their forecasts. In the variants space, you can see things that have never happened, as well as things that will never actually happen.

In this sense, you may rest assured. No one can truly know your future because no one can determine which potential version of it will ultimately be played out on the material plane. Similarly, there is no guarantee that what you see in a dream is the actual sector of the variants space that will be embodied in reality.

This is wonderful news. If the future is not predetermined, there is always reason to hope for the best possible outcome. The task of Transurfing is not to look regretfully at the past or even to peer apprehensively into a tomorrow which is yet to come but to shape intentionally your own reality.

It might seem difficult to believe. Just where is the variants space? How can this be possible? From the point of view of our three-dimensional perception of the world, the variants space is everywhere and at the same time, nowhere. It could lie beyond the visible universe, or it could be in your coffee cup. One thing is for certain; it is not in the third dimension.

Paradoxically, we visit the variants space every night. Our dreams are not illusions in the usual sense of the word. People light-heartedly attribute their dreams to the realm of fantasy, not suspecting that they reflect real events, which might have occurred in the past or might still occur in the future.

We know that people sometimes see images in dreams that do not seem to originate in this world. Or at least, it is quite clear, that the dreamer can't have seen their dream content in real life. If a dream is our brain's way of imitating reality, where do all these extraordinary pictures and narratives come from?

If we roughly attribute all conscious aspects of the human psyche to the mind, and all its subconscious aspects to the soul, then we could say that a dream is the soul's flight through the variants space. The mind does not imagine dreams; it actually sees them.

The soul has direct access to the information field, where all 'scripts and set designs' are permanently stored like frames on a filmstrip. The phenomenon of time only manifests when the 'filmstrip' is moving. The mind acts as an observer and 'ideas generator'.

Memory is also directly related to the variants space. It has already been proved that the brain is not physically capable of storing all the information a person accumulates during their lifetime. So how does the brain remember things?

The brain does not store the information itself; it stores something akin to an address to where the data is held in the variants space. The reason people don't remember their past lives is that when the physical body dies those addresses are lost. Under certain conditions, however, the address files can be restored.

The mind is not capable of creating anything fundamentally new. It simply constructs a new version of a house from old building blocks. The material for any scientific discovery or masterpiece of art comes from the variants space and is received by the mind through the heart. Clairvoyance and intuitive knowledge come from the same place.

«A discovery in science», Einstein wrote, «is not accomplished in any logical way. It only takes on logical form afterwards, in the course of exposition. A discovery, even the very smallest, is always an insight. The solution comes from outside, as unexpectedly as if someone had whispered it in your ear.»

The concept of the variants space should not be confused with the well-known concept of a common information field, through which data can be transferred from one object to another. The variants space is a stationary matrix, a structure that determines everything that can potentially take place in our world.

When we accept the simultaneous existence of two aspects of reality, the physical and the metaphysical, then our picture of the world becomes much clearer. When these two aspects of reality come into contact on the surface of the mirror, phenomena arise that are usually attributed either to the paranormal or unexplained mysteries.

Corpuscular-wave dualism in which a microscopic object is perceived as either a wave or a particle is a vivid example of these two realities coming into contact with one another.

16

However, human beings are the most incredible example of this phenomenon, living creatures, who simultaneously combine the material and the spiritual. In a sense, we are living on the surface of a giant, dual mirror, on one side of which lies our material universe, and on the other stretches the black infinity of the variants space.

Finding ourselves in this unique position, it would be, at the very least, short-sighted to confine ourselves to living within the confines of the conventional worldview making use of just one aspect of reality, the physical aspect.

Given the right conditions, human thought energy is capable of materialising any sector of the variants space. In the state of being referred to in the context of Transurfing as the unity of heart and mind, an unfathomable, magical power is born, the power of outer intention.

Everything that is customarily attributed to magic is connected to outer intention. This is the power the ancient mages used to erect the Egyptian pyramids and create other miracles.

Intention is referred to as 'outer' because it exists external to the individual human being and, as a result, lies beyond the mind's control. That said people are capable of gaining access to it in certain states of consciousness. Anyone who subordinates their will to this powerful force becomes capable of incredible things.

However, in the contemporary world, most people have long lost the skills honed by the inhabitants of ancient civilisations like Atlantis. Fragments of ancient knowledge have been preserved to the present day in the form of scattered esoteric teachings and practices but it is quite difficult to apply this kind of knowledge in everyday life.

Despite the intricacy of its practical realisation, the secret to mastering outer intention is fairly simple. The answer to the enigma lies in the phenomenon known as lucid dreaming.

In an ordinary dreaming state, events develop independently of the mind's will. Until the dreamer becomes conscious of the fact that they are dreaming, they are not able to control what happens. The dreamer is totally under the power of non-lucid dreaming in which the dream just 'happens' to them.

The moment the dreamer becomes conscious of the fact that it is all just a dream; they discover that they have amazing abilities. The impossible is possible in a lucid dream. You can control events in the dream by the power of intention and do incredible things, like fly.

The ability to control one's dream is acquired the moment a person becomes conscious of himself or herself in the dream world comparative to physical reality. At this stage of awareness, the dreamer has their physical reality as a reference point to which they can return the moment they wake up.

Physical reality, in turn, is like a non-lucid dream in waking. The dreamer is under the power of circumstance and life just 'happens'. They don't remember their past lives and so they have no reference point relative to which, they could rise to the next level of awareness.

Yet not all is lost. There is an alternative method in Transurfing, which you can use to get outer intention to work.

People are capable of creating their own reality but this means following certain rules. The ordinary human mind tries to influence the reflection in the mirror but is unsuccessful. It is the image itself that has to be changed, and the image is created by the focus and nature of a person's thoughts.

Desire alone is not enough to bring what you want into reality. The image or thought form on one side of the mirror has to coincide with certain parameters of the corresponding sector of the variants space, located on the other side of the mirror. But that is not all. You have to know how to communicate with the mirror, which, it has to be said, is most strange and complex.

Imagine this unusual scenario. You are standing in front of a mirror but there is nothing in the reflection, just emptiness. The image gradually begins to appear but only after some time, as in a photograph that is being developed. At some point, you begin to smile but the mirror still reflects the former serious expression on your face.

This is exactly how the mirror of the variants space works, only the delay factor is incomparably greater, and therefore the changes that take place cannot be clearly perceived. Material realisation is inert, but if you fulfil certain conditions, a new reflection will appear, which means that a dream can become a reality.

Your thought form acts like an existing physical object that is standing in front of a mirror. Your reflection, which has no material substance, is imaginary, metaphysical and at the same time, as real as the form itself. Unlike the scenario with an ordinary mirror,

19

in Transurfing, the material world is the reflection. The images in it, which are served by the intention and thoughts of God, as well as all living beings, are His manifestations.

The variants space is a kind of matrix, a template for 'cutting' and 'sewing' as well as a format for the 'fashion show,' the movement of all matter. It stores information about what should happen in the material world and how. Each possible variation of potential reality represents a different sector of the variants space, which contains scripts and set designs for the trajectory and form of moving matter. In other words, the sector determines in each individual case what should happen and what that should look like.

Therefore, the mirror divides the world into two halves, the actual and the imaginary. Everything that acquires material form resides in the actual half and unfolds in accordance with the laws of natural science. Science and the ordinary perception of the world deal only with what happens 'in reality'. By reality, it is generally accepted to mean everything that can be observed and directly influenced.

When we reject the metaphysical side of reality and only take into account the material world, the activities of all living beings, including man, are reduced to primitive movements within the confines of internal intention. Internal intention helps us achieve our goals by means of directly influencing the world around us. In order to achieve something, we have to take certain steps, we push, shove, elbow our way ahead and generally carry out a specific type of work.

Material reality instantly responds to direct action, which creates the illusion that results can only be achieved by direct influence. However, in the context of the material world, the range of goals that are realistically achievable using this approach is greatly narrowed. Here, we can only rely on what is already available to us. Everything comes down to material resources, which as a rule, are never enough, and which are severely limited.

In this world, everything is imbued with the spirit of rivalry. There are just too many people wanting to achieve the same thing. Of course, within the limits of internal intention, there really is not enough. So where can we find the conditions and circumstances necessary to achieve our goals? The answer is, only in the variants space.

On the other side of the mirror, everything exists in abundance and there is no competition. None of the products is in stock but the beauty of it is that you can choose anything at all as if from a catalogue and place an order for what you want. Sooner or later, your order will be delivered and you will not even have to pay for it; you just have to fulfil certain straightforward conditions, and that's it. Sounds like a fairy tale?

Not at all! It is more than realistic. Thought energy never disappears without trace. It is capable of materialising any sector of the variants space whose characteristics correspond to the quality of the thought waves being emitted. It only appears to us as if everything in the world were a result of interaction between material objects. Equally important here is the role played by processes which occur on the subtle planes, when virtual variants of potential reality become embodied in physical reality. The causal relationships involved in subtle processes cannot always be perceived, and yet together they comprise the better half of reality.

The physical embodiment of sectors within the variants space takes place, as a rule, irrespective of individual will since people so rarely use thought energy in a purposeful way, to say nothing of less intellectually developed beings.

A person who is firmly grounded in the 'realities of life' is like a shopper, who wanders along empty shelves in a store stretching up to reach for goods which are already marked 'sold'. There are only poor quality products left and even those are expensive. Instead of just looking at the catalog and placing an order, they rush about randomly searching for things, waiting in long queues, desperately struggling to squeeze through the crowd and getting involved in conflicts with the shop keepers and other customers. As a result, they don't get what they want and end up with more problems than they started with.

Meanwhile, this grim reality germinates in that person's consciousness and gradually ends up materialising into reality. All living beings create the layer of their personal world with their actions on the one hand and their thoughts on the other. All these individual layers arrange themselves, one on top of the other, as every living being contributes to the creation of the wider reality.

Each layer is made up of a specific set of conditions and circumstances, which produce a person's life style. The individual conditions of each person's life differ. They may be favourable or unfavourable, comfortable or severe, inviting or aggressive. Naturally, the environment in which a person is born bears some significance. Yet, how a person's life develops will depend for the most part on that person's relationship to themselves and their environment. A person's attitude to life is largely determined by subsequent changes in lifestyle. The sector, scripts, and set designs that most correspond to the focus and quality of a person's thoughts are those, which will ultimately be made manifest in material reality.

Two factors play a part in the process of creating an individual layer: internal intention on one side of the mirror and outer intention on the other. People can influence objects in the material world through action; with their thoughts, they bring into physical reality things, which are not yet there.

When a person is convinced that all the best of this world has already sold out, their shelves will remain empty. When they think that buying a high-quality item will mean standing in a huge queue and then parting with a large sum of money, then that is exactly what will happen. If a person's expectations are pessimistic and riddled with doubt, then they will undoubtedly be justified. If a person expects to meet with an unfriendly environment, their misgivings will come true. Yet all a person has to do is embrace the innocent thought that the world has saved the best for them, and for some reason, that works as well. That is how people shape the layer of their personal world with the power of thought. For the most part though, people don't understand how it all works.

People try to make everything 'exactly how I want it' by applying the basic principle of, 'wherever I turn, that's where I'll go, and wherever I put my foot on the gas, that's where I'll make a breakthrough'. Yet for some reason, the world does not want to yield to this principle. What is more, when a person turns in one direction, life carries them off in quite another.

It makes you think. Given that reality behaves in such a strange manner, perhaps we should take a different approach. What if life works in accordance with completely different laws?Yet people do not want to stop and look around so they continue to push hard ahead.

The result of this kind of 'creativity' is that you end up with a world layer in which 'nothing is how I want it to be'. In fact, quite a lot turns out just 'as I didn't want it to'. How strange, moody and unaccommodating reality is!

One often gets the feeling that the world is doing it out of spite. Trouble seems to be drawn to us by some inexplicable magnetic force. Our fears are realised and our worst expectations justified. We are persistently followed by the very things to which we are adverse, and so try to avoid. Why?

The theory of Transurfing explains why it often turns out that, «You get what you didn't want», especially if you desperately didn't want it. Is there something you hate or fear with all your heart? Outer intention will give it to you in abundance.

The energy of thoughts, which are born from the unity of heart and mind, transform potential into reality. In other words, the sector in the variants space that corresponds to the quality of our thought waves can be materialised, if the feelings of the heart are one with the thoughts of the mind.

This is not the only reason our worst expectations are realised. A problem-free life is actually the norm. Everything in life should develop smoothly if you go with the variants flow and do not upset the balance. Nature does not like wasting energy and has no desire to create intrigue.

Unfortunate circumstances and events occur as a result of excess potential, which introduces an element of distortion into the energetic environment. Dependent relationships only exacerbate the problem.

Excess potential arises when some quality or another is attributed excessive, inflated importance. Dependent relationships are created when people begin to compare themselves, to compartmentalise and set conditions like: "If you do that, then I'll do this".

Excess potential is not necessarily a problem, as long as the distorted evaluation exists relative only to itself. As soon as the artificially elevated evaluation of one object is placed in comparative relationship to another, polarisation crops up which creates a wind of balancing forces.

Balancing forces try to neutralise the polarisation and, in the majority of cases, their impact is focused on the person creating it.

These are examples of unconditional potential: I love you; I love myself; I hate you; I don't like myself; I am good; you are bad. These judgements are self-sufficient. They are not based on comparison or contradistinction.

Here are some examples of potentials built on dependent relationships: I love you provided that you love me; I love myself because I am better than the rest of you; you are bad because I am better than you; I'm good, because you are bad; I do not like myself because I'm worse than anyone else; you repulse me because you are not like me.

There is a huge difference between the first group and the second. Value judgments based on comparison create polarisation. Balancing forces try to neutralise the heterogeneity by the collision of opposites. It is exactly the same as when the opposite poles of a magnet attract.

This is why trouble creeps into our lives so intrusively, as if on purpose. For example, seemingly incompatible individuals unite as a married couple as if they were trying to punish one other. In any team, there will always be that one person you find particularly irritating. Murphy's law or what we would call 'Sod's Law' is the same principle.

Polarisation distorts the energetic environment and generates vortices of balancing forces, as a result of which, reality is poorly reflected as if in a distorting mirror. People do not seem to understand that the problem has arisen because of something that is upsetting the balance, and so they decide to fight the outside world, rather than eliminating the source of polarisation.

All it really takes is to fulfil the basic rule of Transurfing: give yourself permission to be yourself and allow others to be different. You have to let the world go completely, wherever it likes. Loosen your grip.

The more you insist on your own desires and claims, the stronger the magnet that attracts the opposite. This is what happens, literally: you grab the world by the throat and so it fights back, trying to free itself.

There is no point in pushing and demanding. That only exacerbates the situation even more. Instead, the rule of Transurfing requires that you consciously change your attitude towards the situation.

The fact that Sod's Law even exists is a bit odd, don't you think? Why should the world behave in such a bitchy manner? Or does it all come down to speculation and prejudice? There is no getting away from it; the tendency does exist. Fortunately, the Transurfing model not only reveals the reason for this pattern, it explains how it can be avoided.

The rule of Transurfing works flawlessly, and anyone who follows this rule will be freed from experiencing the kinds of problems that seem to appear in our lives without any particular reason. All you have to do is loosen your grip, stop 'grabbing life by the throat' and you will find it instantly becomes friendly and willing.

Those who don't 'let go' will carry on like a magnet, attracting the opposite. The law of bad luck is not the only thing. The moment that opposites meet, their opposition strives to intensify further.

The well-known law of the unity and conflict of opposites, whose title is self-explanatory, is now basic textbook knowledge, just like 'the Volga flows into the Caspian Sea, and the Mississippi into the Gulf of Mexico'. But it's not quite that simple. Ask yourself, why should this law even exist?

The reason for the ubiquitous union of opposites is clear: by making them collide, balancing forces restore equilibrium. So why are opposing elements in a constant state of conflict?

You would think it would be the opposite; they collide, neutralise each other and calm down, but no, opposites go on 'provoking' each other until they get the opportunity to 'fight'. Unless the bully is dragged away, the fight will go on forever.

There's no shortage of examples. You know that life sometimes gets on your nerves a bit. Everyone experiences this in his or her own way to varying degrees. Basically, the essence is this: if right now there is something that is capable of throwing you off balance, it will appear as if to spite you.

This is what happens: If you are anxious, worried or down about something, your nerves will be tense, even just a little. Then, as if it were directly connected, a clown appears and starts jumping about and rattling on, winding you up even more. You get even more irritated and the clown jumps about even more frantically.

There are many ways of increasing your tension. For example, you are in a hurry and afraid you are going to be late. The clown claps and rubs its hands and cries: «Let's go!»

From this moment on, everything starts to go against you. People block your way. They stride along with decorum but you still cannot pass them. You rush to get through a door but there is literally a queue forming of the laziest people in the world who are barely placing one foot in front of the other. The cars on the road are doing the same thing. It is as if they have all agreed beforehand to get in your way.

Of course, some things can be put down to perception. When you are in a hurry the rest of the world seems to slow down but the real telltale signs are when the lift breaks down, the bus is late and there's a traffic jam. In all this, there is some ill-intentioned objective tendency.

I could cite other examples. If you are concerned about something and tense, people around you will always do exactly what irritates you and they seem to know to do it now, when you would most like to be left alone.

The children start misbehaving although they were fine before. Someone sitting next to you starts slurping and swallowing loudly. Various individuals get under your feet and pressure you with their problems. Interference importunately creeps in everywhere. If you wait impatiently, you will wait for ages. If there is someone, you particularly do not want to see, they will appear, and so on.

The more irritated you become, the more the external pressure intensifies. The more tense you are, the more people will get to you. The interesting thing is that they are not actually doing it deliberately. It would never occur to them that they might be bothering someone. So why this behaviour?

There are all sorts of grey areas in the psychology of the subconscious. However strange it might sound, in the majority of cases, people are driven by unconscious motives. What is even more interesting is that the driving force, which shapes our unconscious motives, originates in the external world, not in the human psyche.

This force comes from pendulums, unseen but very real energy-informational entities which are created by thought energy. We talked a lot about pendulums in the first book on Transurfing. Pendulums can always be found in places where they can survive on conflict energy.

It is not that these beings are capable of plotting anything or realising a consciousness intention. Pendulums are like leeches. They sense polarisation as inhomogeneity or lumpiness in the energy field and feed by sucking on it, and that's not the worst of it.

What is so horrific is that rather than just absorbing conflict energy, they somehow push people to behave in such a way that they give out even more of the same type of energy.

They do everything possible to make sure that the source of energy is spilling over. Pendulums pull at people with invisible threads as if they were puppets and they obey. How precisely pendulums influence people's motives is not yet clear, but they are extremely good at it.

Pendulums cannot access clear consciousness but they don't need to; the subconscious is quite enough. To one degree or another, everyone is partially asleep in waking life. We often do things in a laid-back manner, on autopilot, without being aware of it, without saying to ourselves "in this moment I am awake and am aware of what I am doing, why I am doing it and how."

Our level of active awareness is particularly low when we are at home or when we find ourselves in a crowd. In a domestic setting, the need for heightened self-control is relatively minor and so we are relaxed, almost dropping off. In the external world, within a close circle of friends, our awareness is more alert and working on self-control. In large crowds, a person's actions are spontaneous but also fall into strong correlation with the general urges of the collective.

To illustrate how a pendulum works, let's take the simple example of a passerby, who you follow and then overtake. Just as you intend to step to the side to walk past, the pedestrian takes a spontaneous step to the side as if deliberately blocking your way. You try and pass them on the other side but the pedestrian automatically veers in that direction.

What causes the passerby to change direction? They can't see you, and why should they care that you want to pass by? Perhaps the pedestrian senses someone approaching from behind and instinctively stops his or her 'rival' from passing and getting ahead? This explanation would seem viable but, still, that's not it. In nature, if you think in terms of instinct, rivalry is always expressed in situations where both parties are stood facing each other. What makes the pedestrian veer to one side is the pendulum.

People just walk, without thinking about where they are placing their feet or how to keep a perfectly straight line. In this sense, people are asleep, and so from time to time, the line of their steps spontaneously deviates to one side or another. The motivation, the choice to move in one direction or another originates in the subconscious, which in that moment is not being controlled by the mind, which means, it is open to the pendulum.

31

Then you come along and try to overtake the pedestrian in front of you. Essentially, this is a conflict, albeit a very meagre one. The pendulum's objective is to increase the energy of conflict and so it nudges the pedestrian to take an involuntary step to one side, to block your way aggravating the situation further.

You cannot say that the pendulum is acting deliberately because it is not capable of conscious intention. Balancing forces act just as unconsciously. I should emphasise, that we are talking about certain processes of which the precise mechanism is still unclear and not about the rational behaviour of conscious beings. We are simply noting individual tendencies and patterns in the energy-informational world.

There is no point in analysing what kind of pendulum is working in this kind of situation, where it comes from, how it manages to do what it does, and what is really happening on an energetic level. We would never get to the bottom of it. Only one main conclusion concerns us here: when balancing forces make opposites collide, the pendulums do everything to inflame the energy of rising conflict. *That is the law of the pendulum.*

Endless pendulum battles, be they domestic arguments or armed conflicts, all run according to this law. When opposition arises, events will always develop to intensify the conflict and that includes temporary and feigned attempts at reconciliation.

When the pendulum law is at play, common sense has no weight at all. This is why very often common sense seems to have no bearing on the actions of individuals or states. *In conflict situations, a person's motives come under the pendulum's power.*

That is why when you look back on how you have behaved in the past, you often find yourself thinking how strange it all was and wondering what on earth happened to your common sense. You ask yourself, "What could have possessed me to do such a thing?" The answer is that we sometimes come from the subconscious without being fully aware of what we are doing. It is only later, when our consciousness is free of external influence that events can be evaluated more objectively.

People who have been close start to argue and then part ways because they think they are incompatible despite the fact that they have shared many happy times together when everything was wonderful between them. All of a sudden, a person changes and their behaviour becomes hostile. They are not like how they used to be, even in relatively recent times. Sounds familiar, right?

In reality, it is not a matter of one partner or the other has changed. The reason one person behaves in a manner their partner finds totally unacceptable is because the pendulum is forcing them to behave that way.

The pendulum controls the subconscious motivations of people who find themselves in a confrontation. The control is designed to increase conflict energy. Generally, people are unaware of what pushes them to go on the offensive. A person might behave totally illogically or abnormally.

This effect is quite evident in inexplicably brutal crimes. Later, when they are sitting in the dock, the offender recalls their crime in horror wondering: "What on earth came over me?" They are not lying either.

Often the crime is a complete surprise to the perpetrator, who remembers what they did as if it were some terrible nightmare.

The sleep is particularly deep when a person's attention falls into a snare. In certain communities, like in the army, a club or sect, an environment is created which supports a certain type of thinking and behavioural stereotypes. This 'lulls a person to sleep', which makes their subconscious susceptible to the zombifying influence of the pendulum. Then certain things happen which would seem utterly incomprehensible to any objective observer.

Why do people kill others so viciously, simply because they worship different gods? They're not getting in anyone else's way. People suffer deprivations of war and die in dozens, the hundreds, thousands and millions. Where is their preservation instinct? Fighting for the sake of wealth and land is understandable but how do you explain killing for the sake of one's faith?

The idea of peace is close to everybody's heart, and yet the wars continue. The idea of a one God is quite clear. The notions of goodness, justice, equality (one could go on forever) are the same. Everyone understands but common sense doesn't seem to work and evil triumphs. Where does the evil come from?

The pendulum is the universal source of evil. In a confrontational situation involving anything or anyone, you don't have to observe for long before it becomes obvious that events are moving towards an increase of conflictual energy. If the battle ceases, then it will not be for long and only so that it can flare up again later with renewed strength.

Of course, pendulums come in all sorts of guises but they are all destructive to varying degrees. Some are relatively harmless. The purpose of the Transurfing pendulum, for example, is to make as many people as possible think about what is really happening.

It is not a question of freeing ourselves from pendulums altogether. That would hardly be possible. The main thing is not to let yourself be a puppet, to be aware in your actions and to use these structures to your own advantage. So how can we free ourselves from their influence?

Waking up and being aware of how a pendulum is trying to manipulate you and understanding what is really happening is already half the battle. The power of the pendulum's influence is inversely proportional to awareness. The pendulum only has power over you whilst you are falling asleep in waking life.

Most importantly, do not get involved in destructive pendulum battles unless it serves you personally in some way. If you are in a crowd, you need to come down from the stage of action into the audience hall, look around you and wake up. Ask yourself, "What am I doing here? Am I fully aware of what's happening?"

"Why am I here?"

The moment of waking up from sleeping in waking life should be absolutely clear, like the phrase used above, *"In this moment I am awake and fully conscious of what I am doing, and why and how I am doing it."* If you maintain this level of awareness, everything will be alright. If you do not, then in any conflict, even the most minor, you will be the puppet.

Things get much more difficult when something is annoying you. In this case, the clown will keep jumping about until your nerves are strained. This usually means that the pendulum has caught your attention in a snare. In order to free yourself from the pendulum, you need to become indifferent although this can be difficult to do.

For example, the neighbours' music is driving you mad. Your task is to 'unhook' yourself from the pendulum at all cost. It is almost impossible to force yourself out of reacting. There is no point in trying to suppress your emotions. Instead, turn your attention to something else.

Try listening to your own music, not too loudly but just loud enough to drown out the neighbours' music. Think of other ways to distract yourself. If you manage to occupy your thoughts with something else, the neighbours will gradually mellow out.

The same principle applies in other situations too. If the 'clown is dancing', your attention has been caught in some kind of snare. You have been caught up in the pendulum's game whose goal is to increase the energy of conflict. *In order to free yourself from the snare, you have to shift your attention.*

Generally speaking, things are not that bad. Nothing will happen 'to spite you' as long as you aren't sleeping in waking life. You might think that all the above sounds quite ridiculous. It's not easy getting used to the idea that certain entities can control you. Whether you accept this knowledge or not is a matter of personal choice. You don't have to believe it. Simply observe and then draw your own conclusions.

That is a brief summary of the concept of Transurfing. If in the process of working with the Transurfing principles, you come across something you don't understand, you can always refer to the source material, the book in five volumes, *Transurfing Reality*.

Transurfing Principles

1. Awakening

Principle

Wake up, right here, right now! Be aware and remember that everyone is a dreamer and everything that is happening around you is nothing more than a dream, only the dream no longer has any control over you. Now that you have woken up in the dream, you can influence how events will unfold. Your advantage lies in awareness. Feel your strength. Strength is always yours when you remember it. From now on, everything will be as you want it to be.

Interpretation

Your birth into this life represents a new awakening after a series of past incarnations, dreams about reality. From the moment you appeared in the world, you have had amazing abilities. You could hear the rustling of the morning stars, see auras and communicate with birds and animals. The entire world was an astonishing extravaganza of luminous energy and you were the magician, capable of controlling it. However, you soon fell once again under the influence of others and were plunged into a dream. The dreamers constantly and intentionally focused your attention on the physical aspect of reality. As a result, your magical abilities were lost. Have you ever felt as if life were a dream in which reality is controlling you, rather than you controlling it? The time has come to reclaim your former power.

2. Hacking the Dream

Principle

Right now, embrace the awareness that your life is a game, which you have been pushed into playing. While you are mentally engrossed in the game, you can't objectively evaluate a situation or influence the course of events in any significant way. So first, come down into the audience hall, take a good, calm look at everything around you and say to yourself, "In this moment, I am fully awake and aware of where I am, what is happening, what I am doing and why". Then walk back onto the stage and continue playing your role while remaining the witness, like any other member of the audience. Now you have a huge advantage -awareness. You have hacked the game and acquired the ability to control it.

Interpretation

When you dream, you are at the mercy of circumstance. The rational mind sleeps and accepts everything at face value as if everything were unfolding as it should. Waking life is pretty much the same. You might tend to think that reality is something that exists independently, and that you are powerless to influence it.

You are mostly resigned to your lot, the set of capabilities given to you and the conditions of the environment in which you have to exist. All you can do is go with the flow that of fate, from time to time, making minor attempts to assert your rights. Is it really possible to change things? Too right, it is! And you will. Until now, you have probably perceived reality as you were taught to. Now, be aware that reality is like a dream. You can only control the situation through lucid dreaming. On stage, everyone is playing a role and all the actors are interacting with you in one way or another. They might expect something of you, make impositions, requests and demands; they may help, obstruct, love or hate you. Look at the game consciously, from a distance, and then you will understand it all.

3. Child of God

Principle

There is a small particle of God in every one of us. You are a child of God and your life is God's dream. By shaping your own reality with the power of intention, you fulfil God's will. Your intention is God's intention. As this is the case, how can you doubt that your intention will be realised? All it takes is to claim the right. When you ask God for something, it is just the same as if God had asked something of himself. Can God really ask something of his or her self? Is there any one person alive from whom God would ask for something for himself or herself? God just takes what he (she) wants. Do not ask, demand or strive. Shape your own reality by way of conscious intention.

Interpretation

The world is a theatre of dreams in which God is simultaneously a member of the audience, an actor, a scriptwriter, and a producer. As a member of the audience, God observes the play that is unfolding on the stage of the world. As an actor, God feels and experiences everything in the same way as the character whose role he (she) is playing. God creates and controls reality through the intention of all living things. God placed a part of his will together with the soul in every living being and then sent them out into the dream, into life. God gave every living soul the freedom and power to create their own reality by the measure of their awareness. Practically all living beings omit to use the power of intention consciously and with clear purpose. In a state of non-lucid dreaming, it is as if they are vaguely aware of wanting something without really knowing what exactly. Their intentions are therefore blurred, vague and mostly unconscious. In this respect, man has developed little more than animals. The pendulums have not only succeeded in taking away people's awareness of their own abilities, they have perverted the very meaning of life, replacing the notion of being used of God, with worship, whereas in fact, the true goal of life and the idea of service of God consists in co-creation, creation together with God.

4. A Star Is Born

Principle

In order to achieve real success, you have to stop following widely accepted stereotypes and walk your own path. Anyone who pulls out of the general system creates a new measure of success. Pendulums cannot bear individuality. They spot a rising star and have no choice but to make of them a favourite. Once a new rule has been established, the ranks make a U-turn and start following the rising star. In order to establish your own rules, you have to be yourself. You can do it. You simply have to claim the privilege. Only you can decide what privileges you may or may not enjoy.

Interpretation

People spend their entire lives being told they are far from perfect, and that success, wealth and fame are the inheritance of the elite. Pendulums do not deny that anyone can succeed but they do carefully hide the fact that everyone has their own unique qualities and abilities. For the pendulums, individuality is like death itself. If all its adherents were to become free individuals shaking off the strings of control, the pendulum would simply fall apart. Stars are born independently but the pendulums light them up. The role model, the standard of success, is created intentionally, to drive the aspirations of the mass in one direction. In other words, the pendulum's task is to drive everyone into a single rank and force them to obey a common rule. You will achieve nothing until you realise that you have to step out of the rank and file. There is no point in playing someone else's game where you are not the one making up the rules. Whatever you do, always initiate your own game. This is the secret of success.

5. The World Mirror

Principle

The world is what you think of it. The world is a mirror that reflects your relationship to it. Life is a game in which the world puts the same riddle to all its inhabitants: "Ok, guess, what do I look like?" Everyone responds in their own way according to their own perception: "You are aggressive," or "you are cozy," or even "cheerful, gloomy, friendly, hostile, happy, ill-fated." The interesting thing is that in this quiz, everyone is a winner. The world agrees with everyone and appears before each according to the guise that was ordered. What do you think of your world?

Interpretation

When a person is convinced that all the best things in this world have already sold out, their shelves will remain empty. When they think that buying a high-quality item will mean standing in a huge queue and then parting with a large sum of money then that is exactly what will happen. If a person's expectations are pessimistic and riddled with doubt, then they will undoubtedly be justified. If a person expects to meet with an unfriendly environment, their misgivings will be proven true. However, when a person is imbued with the innocent thought that the world has reserved the best in life for them, this also works. The eccentric, who does not know that nothing can be achieved without a struggle, somehow finds himself or herself at the counter, where there has just been a fresh delivery as if timed especially for them. Then they suddenly learn that the first buyer gets everything for free. A long queue forms behind them of people who know that the reality of life is pretty miserable and all the other fools were just lucky. If someday when confronted with the 'realities of life' the lucky eccentric changes their opinion of the world, their reality will change accordingly and when they finally "open their eyes to the truth," they will be thrown right to the very back of the queue.

6. The Boomerang

Principle

Whatever thoughts you send out into the world, they will return to you like a boomerang. What happens when you hate something? You put your heart and mind into a sense of hatred, and this clear, sharp image is reflected in the mirror and fills the entire layer of your world. As a result, you get even more worked up and increase the power of your emotion. In your

44

mind, you feel like sending everyone to hell. "Get lost the lot of you!" But the mirror sends the boomerang back. You tell everyone where to get off and life sends you there instead. Beware of sending negative energy into the world mirror. If you do, you will receive the same response totally unexpectedly. By the way, love is also a boomerang!

Interpretation

Thoughts materialise in the world mirror. For example, if you are not satisfied with your outward appearance, you will take no pleasure in looking in the mirror. You focus all your attention on the features you do not like about yourself and you state them as a fact. You have to understand that how you are reflected in the mirror corresponds to how you feel about yourself. Adopt a new rule; don't look in the mirror, peek in the mirror. Seek out the positive and ignore everything else. Pass everything you see through this filter. Concentrate your attention on the things you want. What did you use to do? You stated facts like, "I don't like myself. I don't like my world." The mirror simply confirmed the fact all the more, "It's true, that's how it is." Now you have a different task. Seek out the things you love and at the same time, picture the desired image in your mind. From now on, all you do is seek out and find signs that confirm evidence of positive change. You'll find that things will get better and better with each passing day. If you practice this regularly, it won't be long before your jaw will be dropping in amazement.

45

7. The Illusory Reflection

Principle

People are like the little kitten that stands in front of the mirror not realising that it is looking at its own image. You might think you are at the hands of circumstance, which you are incapable of changing but this is an illusion, fake prop, which you can easily dispel if you want to. Unconsciously, you are going round in circles. You observe reality and express your relationship to it; the mirror confirms the content of your relationship to reality in waking life. It is like a closed-loop feedback system. Reality is created as a reflection of your thought forms and the nature of the thought form is, in turn, largely defined by the reflection you see in the mirror. The principle of creating your own reality lies in turning the loop in the opposite direction. Look at yourself first and only then in the mirror.

Interpretation

When a person is attached to the mirror by their relationship to the world (a primitive response to reality), they try to chase after the reflection (equally as primitive) in an attempt to change some aspect of it. Now let's try and turn the mirror circle backwards. First, we express our relationship to the world - the mirror consolidates the content of this relationship in reality - and then we observe reality. What do we get as a result?

There is no longer a primitive and powerless assertion about the reflection. This is replaced instead by a deliberate, purposeful assertion of the thought form. Instead of habitually expressing dissatisfaction about what you see in the mirror, turn away from it and start creating a picture in your mind of what you would like to see. That is the way out of the mirror maze. The world first stops and then starts to meet you half way. When you take control of your relationship to reality, outer intention will begin to work, and for outer intention, there is nothing that cannot be realised. All you have to do is switch your attention from the reflection to the image in front of it. In other words, take control of your thoughts. Don't think about the things you don't want and try to avoid; think about the things you do want and are striving to achieve.

8. The Pink Twins

Principle

There are many corners of paradise in the world inhabited by 'Pink Twins'. If you want to go to one of these places, put on your 'rose-coloured glasses' and ignore everyone who tells you to remove them. The echoes of paradise rarely penetrate into everyday life. When they do, catch hold of those 'sun dogs' and keep them in your focus. They will start to appear in your life more frequently and then you will see for yourself how the layer of your world begins unexpectedly to transform.

Interpretation

Have you ever seen it rain on a sunny day? What about two rainbows in the sky? Have you ever crossed paths with twins in pink? It is important to understand one simple thing. Whether you decorate your world in bright, rainbow colours or the darkest of shades depends entirely on your relationship to it. If the majority of your thoughts are related to negative experiences, life will get worse as each day goes by. The opposite is also true. If your soul 'sings in the rain' and 'splashes in the puddles' even when the weather is bad, the layer of your world will be filed with constant celebration. Heaven and hell do not exist somewhere out there in another dimension but here on Earth. There are places like prisons, for example, but that is not where you are; that's not your world, and yet it could become your world if you focus your attention on criminal information. Then there are events like accidents, catastrophes, natural disasters; these too could become part of your reality if you start internalising the news reports. Focus your attention deliberately and solely on the things you want to see in your world. Turn away from everything else. Close your eyes and ears to it all. Evil will never disappear from reality altogether, but it can vanish from your layer of the world. You will simply stop encountering negativity.

9. The Sigh of Relief

Principle

Transurfing is pretty much impossible unless you have relatively high energy levels. As a rule, much of our energy goes on a whole gamut of unrealised plans, which are weighing us down. Goals activate the energy of intention but only if the goal is already in the process of being realised and not a project that just hangs in limbo. It is important either to discard a number of your potential plans or to take steps towards their implementation. Let yourself go. Give yourself more freedom. Make a list of the limitations that are burdening you and shake them off. When you do list, reserves of intention energy will instantly be freed and you will be able to move forward.

Interpretation

Many people go through life, loaded on all sides with the burden of endless responsibilities, unfinished business, harsh conditions, unfulfilled plans and umpteen goals. Take a moment to feel what is weighing you down. If you think about it, you will probably find that you can let go of several lead weights without an ounce of regret. There is no point in constantly dragging them around with you if you can't realise them all. For example, "I have to be better than everyone else; I'll prove to myself and everyone else what I am worth; all I need is victory, otherwise, I'll stop being able to

49

respect myself; I can't afford to make mistakes". And there are others like, stop smoking, learn a foreign language and basically, turn over a new leaf for my entire life on Monday morning. Anything that is endlessly put off until later is excess cargo. An intention must either be realised or discarded because it consumes your energy, which it would be stupid to waste. Is there one big lead weight which you have secretly been thinking of getting rid of but have not yet quite built up the courage to take the step? Imagine how light and relieved you will feel when you have done it.

10. Release

Principle

Life will give you everything you intend to have if you are convinced without reservation that it is rightfully yours. Your choice is law, subject to unconditional fulfilment. Freedom of choice, the determination to have, is created by the energy of intention. If the excess potentials of inner and outer importance consume a significant chunk of your energy, your intention will have no power. In order to let go of the seeming importance of things, be conscious of your actions and aware of the things you attribute inflated importance and the consequences of doing so. The energy of excess potential is dissipated through action. Run your goal slide in your mind and quietly place one foot in front of the other in the direction of your goal. This is all the action you need to take.

Interpretation

How do you stop being afraid? Find a safety net, a fall-back position.

How do you stop being anxious and worrying so much? Take action. The potentials of anxiety and worry are dissipated through action.

How do you stop waiting and wanting? Resign yourself to the possibility of defeat and take action. Dissolve desire and expectation through action.

How do you get over the issue of self-worth? Accept your worth as a statement of fact and let go of any action designed to increase it.

How do you stop getting so irritated? Play with the pendulum and break its game rules. By responding abnormally, you disturb the pendulum's rhythm leaving it with nothing.

How do you let go of feelings of guilt? Stop justifying yourself.

How do you cope with feelings of insult and indignation? Stop fighting and go with the variants flow.

What can you do if you find it impossible to let go of feelings of resentment and anger? Allow yourself this shortcoming. Don't pressure yourself to come always out tops.

Finally, how do you stop yourself from crumbling under the weight of serious problems? Observe the principle of coordinating intention.

Instead of battling with excess potentials, take action on the grounds of purified intention. Intention is cleansed in the process of movement.

11. Confidence

Principle

In order to acquire confidence, you must, first of all, let go of your attachment to the need to be confident. Insecurity lies in overestimating the importance of things. I don't need confidence as a crutch because if I have no importance, I have nothing to protect and nothing to gain. I have nothing to fear and nothing to worry about. If nothing is of excessive importance to me, my world is pure and transparent. I refuse to fight and choose to go with the variants flow. I am empty so I cannot be hooked. I have no need to struggle. I quietly go my own path taking what is mine along the way. This is not a position of shaky confidence so much as a matter of calm, conscious coordination.

Interpretation

Insecurity creates a vicious circle. The more important your goal, the greater your desire to achieve it, the greater the feeling of insecurity. The more worry and anxiety you feel about something, the quicker your fears will prove justified. The battle for self-worth drains your energy. Feelings of guilt can turn a life into the wretched existence of a loser. How do you break out of this tangled maze? You can't. There is no way out. The secret of the maze is that when you stop looking for the way out and let go of the importance of things, the walls of the maze collapse all by themselves. Stop fighting to prove your sense of worth and it will surely be returned to you. Stop justifying yourself to others and you will stop feeling guilty. In the same way, if you reduce the importance you attach to external objects, you will no longer be dominated by their apparent, great significance. Finally, perfect coordination is achieved when the heart and mind are in harmony. To achieve this, listen to the dictates of your heart and stay true to your own beliefs.

12. Balance

Principle

When you find yourself in balance and harmony with the world around you, your life runs smoothly and pleasantly. You achieve your goals without any particular effort. Yet, when you build walls of excess potential, life becomes a battle with balancing forces. When you are faced with a difficult situation, try and recognise where you have gone over the top, what you have become obsessed with, and to what person or thing you might have attributed excessive significance. Define your worth and then let it go. The wall will come tumbling down, the obstacle will remove itself and the problem will be solved of its own accord. Do not try to overcome obstacles. Instead, drop their importance.

Interpretation

Everything in life strives towards balance. Wherever there is excess energetic potential, balancing forces appear with the purpose of eliminating it. When you perceive something as being excessively significant, you get the opposite result to what you intended. For example, when you are critical of yourself you come into conflict with your soul. Balancing forces make you struggle with your shortcomings and try to hide them, as a result of which, they stand out even more. When you are critical of the world, you confront a large number of pendulums. Balancing forces will aim to cut you down to size and push you away. As well as dropping importance, don't push too hard. Reducing outer importance does not mean to disdain things or underestimate them. It is more about not taking life so seriously. Do not disregard things in life, but don't paint them in a saccharine veneer either. Accept the world for what it is. Reducing inner importance is nothing at all like being submissive or self-abasing. Do not embellish or belittle your own strengths and weaknesses. Just give yourself the luxury of being yourself.

13. The Charismatic Soul

Principle

What is the secret of charismatic personalities? They throw the negative slides out of their mind and replace them with positive ones. Charm is a result of the mutual love that exists between the heart and the mind. A charming personality experiences a feeling of joy in their soul; they enjoy life and bathe in their own love without the slightest hint of narcissism. It is this feeling of joy that other people notice. There are not many people like this but you can become one of them. You just have to turn to face your heart, love yourself and step onto the path towards your own personal goal. Not only do certain personal qualities then change but the body becomes more attractive too, the face more appealing and one's smile, absolutely dazzling.

Interpretation

The secret to attractiveness lies in the unity of heart and mind. When a person accepts themselves as they really are, loves themselves and does what they love doing, they radiate an inner light and live their life true to their own credo. This is precisely what people lack and that is why they are drawn to charismatic individuals, like moths to a light bulb. On an energetic level, charm represents pure waves of unity of heart and mind. By training your energy, you develop the extraordinary ability to influence others around you and win them over. A person who has an abundance of free energy generates interest and goodwill in others. If you find it difficult to love yourself unconditionally, start doing an energy field workout by affirming the thought form, "I am spilling over with energy. The intensity of my energy levels is increasing. I have a powerful energy field and it becomes more powerful every day. I shine with the energy of love and charm. I am a pure energy source. People sense my energy field and are well disposed towards me". When you notice people genuinely feeling drawn towards you, don't forget to tell yourself that the technique is actually working. The rational mind needs to hear you affirming it because it is constantly in doubt: "Can I really be capable of that?"

14. Love Yourself

Principle

If you don't love yourself, no one else will, and what's more, you will never be happy. Any conflict between the heart and mind reflects negatively on a person's appearance and character. Correspondingly, the shades of your personal world will turn ever darker. Above all, love yourself, and only then pay attention to the positive qualities of others. It is important to feel and understand the following: pendulums force you to change, to turn away from your heart and follow the rule that states, 'they are better than you, so do what they do, be like them, take your place in the matrix, be nothing more than a cog.' In reality, you are unique. Go inside, accept yourself as you really are, and assert the right to be right. Then you will have something of which you can be proud and a reason to respect yourself.

Interpretation

Once a person has gone a long way down the road of conforming to other people's standards, it is difficult for them to start suddenly loving themselves. "How can I love myself if I don't even like myself?" This is pure excess potential born of inflated inner and outer importance. It is outer importance in that you perceive someone else's standards as the epitome of perfection. Are you not perhaps valuing other people's qualities too highly? Inner importance is present in forcing yourself to follow other people's standards. Who says that you are any less worthy than they are? Is your self-esteem perhaps a little too low? To love yourself, kick outer importance off the pedestal and give up the idol worship. Who is stopping you from setting your own standards? Let others chase after you instead! Drop your own inner importance and let yourself go. Give yourself the luxury of having shortcomings and focus your attention on your strengths.

15. I Am My Goal

Principle

If you have been ditched and are suffering from unrequited love or if you are looking for love, you must, first of all, love yourself. If you do not yet feel that you can love yourself just as you are, start taking care of yourself and focusing on your own personal development: enrol at a sports centre, commit to studying a foreign language, try dressing differently, not in your usual style, get a magic tattoo, find a magic talisman - a pendant or ring. When you start taking care of yourself, you will find a new sense of purpose. Looking after yourself could become your goal if you have not already found one. This is a truly worthy goal and it will bring you success and abundance. You deserve the very best.

Interpretation

It is human nature that people are only pleased with themselves when other people happen to be pleased with them and that they only love themselves when others love them. And yet, the world is a mirror. How can there be love in the reflection if the image itself does not contain it? The mirror cannot reflect what isn't there. It's a vicious mirror circle. So, how do you break it? Very simply. Firstly, it is a well-known fact that we love the people we take care of. So, pay more attention to yourself, take care of yourself, take some 'me time'. Secondly, love is like a boomerang. If you send love out into the world, it will come back to you. You will experience love, including love for yourself if you shine with love instead of emanating fear, mistrust, and disapproval. If you take the first step, the reflection will meet you half way. It is basically a feedback chain: I send love out to the world – love is reflected and comes back to me – the world reciprocates – I am loved – it follows that I like myself too and begin to love myself.

16. Faith

Principle

'According to your faith let it be to you'. This has been said before and more than once, and it really is true. But how do you start believing it? It is useless trying to persuade or convince yourself that it is true. Instead, get down to something concrete i.e. shaping your reality according to the Transurfing principles and visualising your goal slide. Put the principles into practice and you will see what happens. Outer intention will open a door onto the world in which the impossible becomes possible. When the mind is faced with fact, it will include the inconceivable into its worldview and allow a miracle to happen. When you see that Transurfing works, you won't need to have faith. You will have knowledge instead.

Interpretation

Transurfing gives you a map of the territory and the rules of the game. It is up to you, what you decide to do with them. You are the king (or queen) of your personal world. Do not succumb to other's influence. Believe in yourself. Don't rely on other people's decisions. You know better than anyone else what needs to happen and how. Even now that you have knowledge, you will not be immune from making mistakes. True success grows out of the ruins of your failures. Most prominent figures have been through a lot. It is just that these areas of their life tend to be glossed over. So if you have suffered a failure, rejoice, you are on the path to success. Sometimes you will feel as if circumstances are stacked against you and yet, how can you really know, exactly which path will lead you to achieve your goal? The guardians of ancient knowledge have revealed Transurfing not to try and make you believe in the reality of metaphysics but to inspire hope. Where there is faith, there is always room for doubt. We need hope so that we can start to take action. Begin to take action and you will see how things that previously seemed inconceivable begin to manifest into physical reality. When hope has done its work, you will gain awareness. Then you will say to yourself, "I don't wish, I don't believe, I don't hope – I intend and I know."

17. Feelings of Guilt

Principle

The sense of guilt always generates scenarios related to punishment, without you realising it. This is typical of the usual worldview. Every crime is always punished. As soon as you notice the slightest trace of guilt, get rid of that rubbish immediately. Do not let it spoil your life. Live true to your own convictions and you will never experience guilt. No one will dare to judge you if you do not consider yourself guilty. When you are free of guilt, you will never find yourself in a situation in which someone tries to threaten you with violence. No guilt, no punishment.

Interpretation

If you are struggling to shift a guilt complex, it is important to stop justifying yourself. This is one of those cases where treating the symptoms of the disease successfully deals with the cause. You do not have to convince yourself that you are not obligated to anyone. Simply observe your everyday actions. This requires a certain level of awareness. If previously you had the habit of apologising for the slightest thing, adopt a different habit. Explain your actions only when it is absolutely necessary. Stop feeling as though you owe something to others. Even if the feeling of being obligated continues, do not show it outwardly. When they stop getting the former knee-jerk reaction, the manipulators will gradually back off. At the same time, the heart and the mind will gradually get used to the new sensation. If you are not trying to justify yourself, then things are obviously as they should be, and so your guilt simply cannot exist. As a result, the need for 're-demption' will appear less and less often. Therefore, via the feedback chain, the outer form will gradually tidy up the inner content. The feeling of guilt will disappear and with it, all its associated problems.

18. Self-worth

Principle

When a person tries to make themselves seem more important because they feel inferior in some way, the opposite happens. The harder they try to emphasise their worth, the less significant they actually become and vice versa. When a person is not worried about their worth, their sense of worth is unconditional. Our sense of self-worth is a very cunning type of excess potential. Balancing forces will do anything they can to wobble you off your pedestal. When you let go of your own worth, you start to acquire it. At the same time, be careful never to bruise someone else's sense of worth. Make it a personal taboo. If you do, you will save yourself a lot of problems that would seem to come out of nowhere.

Interpretation

The need to strengthen your position and emphasise your finer qualities is an illusion. It's the same as chasing after the reflection in the vicious mirror circle. So how do you convince yourself that you are worthy and have no need to prove it? There is one feedback chain by which the effect removes the cause. You have to redirect your intention consciously. Rather than trying to put yourself forward in the most favourable light, stop making any attempt at all to increase your worth. When a person isn't trying to make themselves appear more important (although almost everyone does it), people intuitively sense that their value goes without saying and that person is, as if by magic, treated with greater favour and respect. As a result, the heart and mind are gradually instilled with the conviction that, «I really am worth something.» At a certain point, the mirror circle stops and then turns in the opposite direction moving towards you. As a result, your self-esteem improves and it is as if you never had an inferiority complex at all.

19. The Master's Credo

Principle

Always be yourself. Don't try and change yourself under any circumstances. Live life according to your own credo. When you contradict your own credo or worse when you simply don't have one, you undermine yourself as an individual and everything in life goes awry. When the image is distorted, the reflection in the mirror is distorted too. It is important to bring your thoughts and actions down to the same denominator: be true to yourself. Then the dual mirror will be free of any crooked distortion. You are the Master of your own reality. You have no reason to feel shame or fear. Remember, you are not alone. The Force is with you, and your world takes care of you.

Interpretation

When you live true to your own credo, the heart and mind come into union. This means, that you take the actions you consider necessary without bothering about social opinion. Never change yourself under any circumstances. If you do feel pushed into doing something, which your soul actively protests against, everything will end up going to pot. Conversely, when you live in accord with your own credo, even if some of your actions seem to contradict common sense, everything will turn out all right in the end. There is no need to analyse exactly how your credo is straightening out reality. It is simply that the lack of distortion in the image makes the reflection normal again. Unity of heart and mind produces a clear image, which instantly materialises in the mirror world. All your true desires will be fulfilled. It is a universal law.

20. Your True Path

Principle

It is not worth setting out on a path that has no 'heart'. This path leads to a complete dissonance between the heart and the mind. You will experience a feeling of uneasiness in your gut, uncertainty, and frustration. On the one hand, it looks as if you are doing everything right and yet, on the other hand, your subconscious tells you that things are not right at all. When a path 'has heart', you will feel it through and through. When you go your own way, you have the incomparable feeling that everything will turn out just as you want it to. It gives you a calm, characteristic confidence. Go your own way, on which the soul rejoices, and your mind rubs its hands in glee. If you intend to find your true path, there is no doubt that you will find it.

Interpretation

When you start living for yourself and doing what you enjoy doing, everything else in your world will catch up to comply with your path. It is all very simple. When heart and mind are in harmony, everything else automatically falls into place. When they are not in harmony, for example, when the heart is asking for something and the mind is afraid, it is important to act cautiously and prudently. Listen to your heart, but remember that you live in a material world, which is not always capable of adapting to your desires instantaneously. Of course, it is not hard to walk away from a job you hate but if you are afraid of being left without an income, do not expect a miracle. If you use the slides technique, you will be able to find any kind of work you want, be it in another city, in another country even, but without reliable support at this stage, you will be too anxious to practise the technique calmly. Never burn your bridges.

21. The Master's Verdict

Principle

Your entire life, people have been telling you how to be, how to behave, what to read and what to strive for. Now, give yourself the lawful right to establish your own cannons. It is for you to decide what is right for you and what isn't because you are the one shaping your personal world. You have the right to determine as true, something that others consider false, so long as it does not harm anyone. When you assume the privilege of passing your own verdict, you are staying true to your own credo. The right to pass the Master's verdict means freedom from oppressive circumstances, from everything that puts a cloud over your life and throws obstacles onto your true path. It will help you acquire a certain calm confidence.

Interpretation

There are as many opinions in life as there are people. Some call it «black,» others call it «white». Whom should you believe? As you will remember, the world is a mirror. It agrees with everyone who dares pass judgment. But you are not a mirror! Either you are the kind of person who accepts other people's verdicts, or you are the Master, who arrives at their own verdict. In this case, which truth you consider the ultimate truth, which side you support, the 'blacks' or the 'whites' is no longer an issue. Now you can decide on your own truth: My decision is this because I am the Master of my own reality. And it will work because you have the variants space and the dual mirror at your disposal, everything you need to manifest your vision into physical reality. There is just one condition: you must have the boldness to exercise your right. If you indulge in self-doubt or have qualms of conscience, your verdict will lose its power and you will be transformed from the lawmaker into the accused. You never take the right action when you doubt yourself. It is not so much a matter of how rightly you think or behave; it's a matter of how confident you are in being right. You mustn't allow the Master's will to become a dictate of the mind. A verdict only has power when the heart and mind are one. Those who fail to listen to their heart never master; they make mistakes.

22. Declaring Intention

Principle

In order to shape reality effectively, you have to try to control your thoughts and not let them run away with you. It can be a bit of a strain at first but with time, it will become a habit. Don't do anything just for the sake of it, mindlessly, floating about in an amorphous jelly of uncontrolled thinking. State your declaration of intention; concentrate on your goal. This does not mean that you have to be permanently on maximum alert. Let your thoughts drift as much as they want to, but be conscious that it is happening: "if my mind is wandering, it is because I am allowing it to". Then, when you need to, return to a state of concentration equally as mindfully.

Interpretation

Usually, the 'thought mixer' works by itself. Ideas emerge and fade uncontrollably and thoughts jump from one theme to the next. The mind 'kicks' just like a baby. So what's the lesson in all this? If you want to create your own reality quickly and effectively, train yourself to say your thought forms to yourself, from time to time throughout the day repeating the narrative for what you want to achieve (it is a good idea to keep your main goal constantly 'in the back of your mind'). By speaking your declaration aloud, you set the course of your intention. For example, adopt the habit of spending a few minutes each day affirming the following thought:

"My brain is fitted with a self-development program. It is constantly developing and perfecting itself. New connections are being made between the left and right hemispheres. Both hemispheres work sharply, coherently and synchronously. I have an incredible mind. Incredible ideas come to me. I think outside of the box. My brain's reserves are contributing to this work. My brain is ninety percent active. I have a fine intellect and it is becoming more powerful every day. I solve problems easily. My awareness is becoming clearer. Everything is transparent and simple. I understand things clearly and express myself clearly."

You can create similar affirmations of your own and repeat them at a set time, after you take a shower or once you've done your workout, etc. Imagine and it will come into being!

23. Resolve to Act

Principle

If there is something, you need or want, do not waste energy procrastinating over it. Just take what is yours as if you had received a card from the post office asking you to collect a parcel. You have to intend rather than deliberate. If what you need, right now is a bus, a parking spot, a purchase, a document, an exam, an interview, a meeting — anything, do not just think about it, go out and get it. Let go of worrying thoughts, such as, 'but is it possible, how will I do it, where will I find it'. Ditch all anxiety, hope, and desire until all that you have left is a calm confidence. Focus on what it feels like to get what you want without all sorts of conditions or reasoning about it. For example, I don't think about whether I'll be in time for the bus, whether the bus will come or how long I will have to wait... I simply walk to the bus stop knowing that the bus will arrive at any moment. Let this state accompany you everywhere.

Interpretation

Usually, when you experience any momentary desire, an analyser switches on in the brain and starts asking, "But will it work or not?" You have to give up this harmful habit. Desires are not fulfiled, dreams do not come true, but pure intention manifests. It is not the desire itself that leads to manifestation but the affirmation of what is desired. Intention is not about intensity or zeal. It is about quite focus and resolve. If you doubt or fear, the world like any mirror will reflect your emotional state, and as a result, nothing will come of what you wanted. Whatever you do, do it with confidence. There is always a possibility of failure. However, your chances of success are greatly increased when you aren't wavering. What do you have to lose by letting go of doubt? If it works out then great, if it doesn't, it's not the end of the world. Support can be found in the principle of coordinating intention. If you turn your thoughts concerning a seemingly negative event into positive thoughts, then that is exactly

what the event will be. Think of consciously controlling your resolve to act as if you were directly controlling your measure of good luck.

24. Resolve to Have

Principle

When there is not a single shadow of doubt, desire
or fear in your mind, just the quiet resolve to have,
then the impossible becomes possible. You can pass
an exam without knowing the subject, sail through the
most gruelling of interviews, secure a super-lucrative
contract, win a hopeless case and charm people you
never dared dream would be in your league. Let go
of the desire to achieve your goal. Be dispassionate
like a Samurai who lives as if his body were already
dead. Be reconciled with the idea of defeat but in your
thoughts, imagine that the goal is already in the bag.
Cast hope aside. Hope is the lot and salvation of the
weak. Have nothing but the willingness to receive it.
That is what you want, right? So what's the problem?
Yours it will be.

Interpretation

Desire is when you focus your attention on the
goal. Internal intention is when you focus your attention on the process of progressing towards the goal.
Outer intention is when you focus your attention on
how the goal is manifesting of its own accord. Inner

intention helps you achieve your goals within the physical world; outer intention selects the goal from within the variants space. Inner intention is aimed at directly influencing the world around us, whereas outer intention allows the goal to be realised in accordance with the intention. Unconditional, unreserved belief in success is what triggers the workings of outer intention. Usually, the mind desires and the soul protests or the soul longs for something and the mind won't bring it into play, as a result of which, the image that stands in front of the world mirror is blurred and indistinct. When the soul and the mind are united in their striving, a clear image is generated which is instantly materialised from the variants space via the mirror. Mean to have what you imagine. You have nothing to lose. Your options are limited only by the clarity of your own intention.

25. World Cleanup

Principle

If you are experiencing burdensome feelings of emptiness, have a good clear up at home or at work. Rearrange your furniture; get rid of accumulated rubbish and old things you no longer need. Then rearrange your possessions you need and value tastefully and with care. You will feel spurred energy and sparked joy. Cast away negative thoughts just as strictly and resolutely, so that they don't sour your world. Fear, anxiety, doubt, negative expectations, dissatisfaction, judgment, resentment, feelings of guilt and inadequacy, clear all this rubbish off your personal planet.

Interpretation

Constructive activity is the best cure for depression. The results are never long in coming. When you are creating something, no matter what that is, the soul regains a lost taste for life. Have a good old tidy up. Taking out the rubbish is a particularly effective remedy for depression. In the same way, clear up your entire personal world. Everyone creates the layer of the world they live in with their thoughts and actions. Your mindset and way of thinking play a fundamental role. Your world will become as you imagine it to be. If you perceive the world as an aggressive, hostile place, then that is how it will show up for you. If you believe that all the benefits of this world are only achieved by putting in a huge amount of effort, you will constantly find yourself having to work really hard. If you believe that wealth and success are the satellites of the elite, you will always find yourself standing at the back of the queue. The more negativity you have swimming around in your mind, the more miserable your reality will be. By getting rid of negative stuff, you will be surprised to find your reality increasingly taking on warmer, cosier shades.

26. Wave of Success

Principle

Perhaps sometimes you feel inspired and on top of the world but then the daily grind brings you back down again. How do you hang on to that feeling that life is a song full of happiness, a celebration? First and foremost, you have to remember how that feels. Keep the sparkle of that feeling of celebration alive and cherish it. Notice your life changing for the better. Grasp at any straw of joy, look for auspicious signs in everything. Never forget, not even for a moment, that you are following a course in Transurfing, consciously going after your dreams, and that means, shaping your destiny. This alone is enough to give you peace of mind, confidence and joy, which means that you are being the magical song of happiness in your life. When feeling wonderful becomes a habit, you will find yourself permanently on the crest of a wave of success.

Interpretation

Be happy and grateful for everything you have in this moment. This is no empty call to be happy by default. Sometimes when circumstances stack up against you, it is very difficult to be content but from a purely practical point of view, there is simply no benefit in expressing dissatisfaction. Don't take bad news to heart. If you don't let it into your heart, you'll keep it out of your life. Close the door on bad news and open up to good news. It is really important to take note of the smallest sign of positive change and nurture it carefully. When your relationship with yourself and the world around you is good, a field of harmonious vibration surrounds you, and everything inside it goes well. A positive attitude always leads to creativity and success.

27. Chasing the Reflection

Principle

How does a person usually respond when they see something manifesting that they do not want in their life? The everyday mind tries without success to manipulate the reflection in the mirror, when in fact, it is the image itself that must be changed. The image represents the focus and quality of our thoughts. Imagine how ridiculous it looks to see a person standing in front of a mirror trying to catch hold of the reflection so that they can create something from it. You have to tear your eyes away from the mirror and let go of the shortsighted intention to turn the world in the direction you want it to go. Purposefully send your thought forms out into the world and adopt a positive attitude. Everything will turn out just the way you want it to.

Interpretation

Make an inventory of your thoughts and eliminate every occurrence of the particle 'not'. Dissatisfaction, reluctance, rejection, disapproval, hatred, lack of belief in your own success and so on, take all this rubbish, shove it in a sack and chuck it on the rubbish heap. Your thoughts should be focused on what you like and want. Then only the good stuff will be reflected in the mirror. On the other hand, be prepared for it to take some time before you begin to observe positive changes in your personal world, or for the opposite to happen with all sorts of unpleasantness creeping in. And what of it? These are all just a temporary inconvenience associated with 'moving' to a new level of relationship with reality. As you know, the mirror works with a delay factor. You have to hold the frame, no matter what. Quietly hold the pause for a bit, while nothing is happening. It's just like in the fairytale when they say, «Don't look back or you'll turn to stone!» I don't know what on earth is going on in the mirror, but I know this, "The mirror has no choice. Sooner or later, it will have to reflect the image I am creating in my thoughts. As long as I stand my ground and am not tempted to look back, the mirror will create My reality. Everything will be the way I want it to be.»

28. Creating an Image

Principle

In order for a thought form to become rooted in physical reality, it has to be reproduced systematically. You might not have thought that the process could be so mundane. It is just ordinary, routine work, nothing to do with magic at all, and yet, it really works. Mostly, people just don't have the patience to keep at it. They experience a surge of enthusiasm when they are first lit up with an idea but as a rule, their excitement quickly fades. For a goal slide to become manifest in physical reality, you have to run it in your thoughts for a fairly long time. There is no such thing as miracles. It comes down to the concrete work involved in shaping reality.

Interpretation

As long as the rational mind is not fighting against the dictates of the heart, the unfathomable power of outer intention will emerge and materialise the sector of the variants space that most closely corresponds to your thought form. When the soul and the mind are united, the image takes on sharp contours and manifests instantly. The world literally agrees with your thoughts about it. So why is it, that as a rule, our worst expectations are justified and our hopes and dreams never come true? In life, what mostly happens is that the mind doubts whatever the soul strives towards and refuses to bring it into play. Or it is the other way around: the mind makes a compelling case for its own project but the heart is indifferent. When unity between heart and mind is lost, the image becomes blurry and appears to split. The heart wants one thing; the mind insists on another. When this happens, they can only fully agree on one thing: resentment and fear. So what can be done? The matter involved in material realisation is inert like resin. A fortress can only be taken by long siege. If you really want to achieve your goal, visualise the slide regularly.

29. World, Give Yourself to Me!

Principle

When you want something from the world, don't pressure the world to give it to you. What else can the mirror reflect when a capricious child is standing in front of it, jumping up and down, crying, "I want it! Give it to me!"

"Yes, you want it, yes you demand it."

The mirror reflects fact, nothing more, nothing less. The principle is very simple. If you want the reflection in the world mirror to meet you half way, you will have to take the first step. Let go of the intention to receive and replace it with the intention to give and you will receive the very thing you let go of in the first place.

Interpretation

Do you want a certain person to acknowledge and respect you? Don't demand it. Show this person respect yourself and make them feel that they are important in your eyes. Do you feel in need of compassion and gratitude? Don't search for it. Take genuine care of someone else and actively help them with their problems. Do you want people to like you? A pair of beautiful eyes won't do it. Show warmth towards someone and they will automatically perceive you as being lovable. Do you need someone's help and support? Find someone to help. You will become more important, and that person, not wanting to be less important than

77

you, won't want to remain in your debt. Do you want to experience mutual love? Let go of possessiveness and dependent relationships. You will experience mutual love if you are prepared to love without receiving anything in return. This kind of love is extremely rare. No one will be able to resist. In all these situations, you are certain to experience the very thing you let go of.

30. Here World, Have Me!

Principle

As a rule, people tend to be entirely consumed by thoughts of what they want from others, without trying to understand what others want for themselves. By shifting your attention to the desires and motives of others, you easily get what you want for yourself. All you have to do is work out where your partner's internal intention is focused. Whenever you need something from a person, to gain their favour or encourage them to do something, ask yourself this question: "What does this person want? What motivates them and what are they interested in?" Direct your actions towards realising your partner's intention and they will willingly reward you with the same.

Interpretation

In one way or another, all the problems we face with other people result from conflicting internal intentions. Motivated by their own interests, people are inevitably trying to get something from someone else while that person is thinking down entirely different lines, focused instead on what's important to them. Use other people's internal intention to achieve your own goals. A person's sense of self-worth lies at the very foundation of their internal intention. Beyond life itself, nothing is more important to a person than his or her own sense of self-worth. Shift your attention from yourself to other people. Stop playing the game of increasing your own worth. Play the game of making other people feel greater self-worth. To attract attention to yourself, it is enough to show interest in others. Don't talk to people about what interests you; talk to them about themselves and the things that interest them. Your personal strengths and weaknesses are what interests your partner least. What they are most interested in is the feeling of self-worth they experience when they are talking to you. How can you motivate some-one to do something? Present the task to them in the light of how it will increase their sense of self-worth and they will be want to be involved.

31. The Oyster Effect

Principle

People tend to gladly express an attitude of discontent, when they feel they have good cause to and yet respond almost indifferently, when something good happens, almost as if they take that for granted. Overall, people are not conscious of this tendency. They are reacting like an oyster, out of habit. Now step up a notch from the oyster. Wake up and make use of the advantage of consciously expressing your relationship to life. "I choose the colours for my personal reality with intention. Irrespective of the circumstances, I attune myself to a major key. I do this consciously rather than reacting in a primitive way to external irritants." By controlling the pattern of your thoughts, you control reality. If you don't, reality will control you.

Interpretation

The tendency to negativity generates all kinds of icky features in the mirror, and then your personal world is painted in gloomy colours and filled with unpleasant events. When a person is depressed, the storm clouds gather all the faster in the mirror reflection. As soon as a person takes an aggressive stance, the world responds by bristling its fur. You may have noticed that when you argue with someone, sharply expressing your position, some other unpleasant event seems to appear out of left field. The more irritated you get, the more insistently trouble sinks its claws into you, the more everything around you starts getting under your skin. What matters, is what you are thinking about, not how you are thinking about it. Whether you like the reflection or not, it is still the subject of your thoughts: «Leave me alone!» or «I've so had enough of all this!» The only thing that matters is the content of your thoughts. As a result, the reflection in the mirror is dominated with things that correspond to the content of the image (your thoughtform). When you take control of the emotions that keep you so attached to the reflection, you free yourself from the mirror. There is no point in trying to suppress your emotions. Your feelings are just a symptom of your relationship to what's going on. You have to change your attitude, how you perceive and respond to reality. When you have freed yourself from attachment to the mirror, then you will acquire the ability to create the reflection you want to see.

32. The Master's Intention

Principle

Using your willpower, you declare any event or circumstance favourable and to your advantage. This affirmation is not merely based on hope in the good-will of the world, which takes care of you because it loves you. It is not derived from trust or confidence, which circumstances can cause to crumble at any moment nor is it born of the arrogance of blind faith in your own success. It is not even based on optimism. It is the Master's intention. You are creating the individual layer of your world and you are the master of your personal reality. You are a Master of reality if you can 'move yourself' at the same time as leaving the world free to move.

Interpretation

The Master is not so much an active figure as a witness. Rather than leading, you allow. That is what makes the Master's intention different. When you look in the mirror, don't try to move the reflection, move the image instead, your attitude and the focus of your thoughts. In other words, 'move yourself' rather than trying to grab hold of the reflection. If you interpret 'intention' as the determination to demand from the world whatever you think it owes you, you will be left with nothing. If you ask the world for what you want, you will still be left with nothing. All you have to do is place your order and allow the world to process it for you. You stop the world from working on your order because you demand, petition, fear, and doubt. Therefore, the world also demands, asks, fears and doubts. It reflects your relationship to life impeccably; after all, it is only a mirror. You have to really feel this truth. Let the world go, allow it to be a comfortable place for you to be, right now. This fragile, fleeting feeling will pass quickly, so you have to hold on to it. Imagine for a moment an incredible thing. Your hostile, problematic, difficult and uncomfortable world has suddenly been transformed into a joyous, comfortable life. You give it permission to be that way. It is up to you to decide. The secret to this power lies in releasing your grip.

33. The Pendulum Rule

Principle

The pendulum rule reads: «Do as I do» which means, change yourself, change yourself and copy the stereotype. In the effort to live up to someone else's standard of success, people lose themselves and become deeply unhappy, because keeping up with all the standards is simply impossible. So, don't do it. Don't be afraid of breaking the pendulum's rule. Set your own standards. Those who violate the pendulum's rule become either leaders or renegades. Some break through to the stars and others turn into outcasts. The difference between the two is that the former act as if they have the total right to break the pendulum's rule and the latter doubt whether they have the right or not. Claim the right to break the rule.

Interpretation

The pendulum's rule is what establishes norms of behaviour and thinking, the standards of 'normality'. People do not understand that they are being offered an ersatz, a surrogate of success. No one individual's success can serve as a model for others to replicate. Only People who dare to break the rules and find their own path in life achieve true success. When you follow other people's example, you are forever doomed to chase the setting sun. Standards of success are a mirage. People do not realise, or do not want to realise that the pendulum is trapping them in a web of illusion. The illusion is often sweeter, more convenient and clearer than the uncertainty of reality. On the other hand, if you do occupy a certain position within a structure, bear in mind, that you cannot just mindlessly antagonise it. It is not a question of freeing ourselves from pendulums altogether. That would hardly be possible. The most important thing is to avoid

83

being a puppet and act with conscious awareness so that you can use the structure in your own interests. Strive to set new rules for yourself, without breaking the system's existing rules.

34. The Transurfing Rule

Principle

Discard the pendulum's rule, «Do as I do» and replace it with the Transurfing rule: «Give yourself permission to be yourself, and allow others to do the same». Giving yourself permission to be yourself means accepting yourself, warts and all. Allowing others to be themselves means withdrawing the expectations you project onto them. This universal rule gives you the chance to find inner freedom and wave goodbye to all sorts of problems that may have plagued your life.

Interpretation

You do not have to worry too much about how the Transurfing rule works. Just follow the rule. Whenever you are faced with a difficult situation, ask yourself: «How can I act in this situation without breaking the Transurfing rule?» This will allow you to solve a whole range of issues: find your inner strength (your personal credo), get rid of the complexes of guilt and inferiority, feel confident, avoid all conflicts and disappointments, unravel intricate knots of the interpersonal conflict and, finally, find your own way in life. The Transurfing rule is the dignity of kings.

35. Dropping Importance

Principle

All unbalanced emotions and reactions like indignation, dissatisfaction, irritation, anxiety, worry, depression, confusion, despair, fear, pity, dependency, lust, over-sensitivity, idealisation, admiration, delight, disappointment, pride, conceit, contempt, repulsion, resentment, and so on, are all the result of overstating the importance of things. Pendulums hook you up on these strings and turn you into a puppet. Dropping importance does not mean battling with your feelings and trying to suppress them. It means addressing the cause, the underlying attitude. You have to reach the point where you can see that importance leads to nothing but trouble. Then, deliberately reduce the importance you attribute to things.

Interpretation

Problems as such do not actually exist. All that really exists is an artificially inflated evaluation of the importance of things. When a person becomes aware that their problems are illusory, they can intentionally reduce the importance of everything that continuously troubles them. Note: Do not play down their meaning, just reduce their importance. Watch the game

85

from a distance, soberly and impartially. By reducing importance, you will instantly return to a state of balance and the pendulums won't be able to control you. In the empty space you free up, there will be nothing for them to hook. This does not mean that you have to have a heart of stone. Emotions are born of our attitude and so it is our attitude which should be changed. Feelings and emotions are just an effect. Importance is the only cause. Let's say that in my family there has been a birth, a death, a wedding or some other significant event. Would the event be important to me? No. Would I be indifferent? Likewise, no. Do you get the difference? I would not publicise the event into a problem or drive myself and others around me mad because of it. A strong deviation towards outer importance breeds fanatics and deviation towards inner importance, idiots.

36. Ending the Battle

Principle

The world is a mirror that reflects your relationship to it. When you are unhappy with the world, it turns away from you. When you battle with the world, it battles with you too. When you stop battling, the world meets you half way. If you simply give yourself permission to have what you envision, outer intention will find a way of giving it to you. Then, one fine day, something will happen that others will call a miracle. Are you desperate to achieve your goal? If so, stop wanting and receive it anyway. Just think about taking what is yours, and taking it quietly, without insisting or making demands in the manner of: «So, I want this. So what? I shall have it.»

Interpretation

Pendulums impose a totally different kind of script. They force you to fight to achieve your goal as if the only means of reaching your goal is to declare war on yourself and the rest of the world. They constantly bombard you with the idea that because you are less than perfect, you will never achieve your goal unless you change who you really are. Once you have changed yourself, then you have to join the battle for your place under the sun. This script pursues one goal only, to drain your energy and drive you into a cell in the matrix. By fighting with yourself, you give your energy away to the matrix. By battling with the world, you do exactly the same thing. No one can force you to fight but you will not have any other option if you are filled with inner and outer importance. If you don't feel able to give yourself permission to take and have right now, you can put it off until later. However, putting it off until later leaves you feeling that every moment of your life is just the preparation for some better future. People are always dissatisfied with the present and console themselves with the hope that improvements are on the cards. With this kind of attitude, the future will never come. It will always be hovering somewhere just ahead of you, like trying to catch up with the setting sun. Give yourself permission to have, right here and now.

37. Co-ordinating Intention

Principle

If you intend to look at events that seem negative in a positive light, then that is exactly what they will be. Remember, however bad things are now, a lovely surprise will come your way on the condition that you maintain coordination in the present moment. When faced with any test in life, tell yourself this: «If it works out, great. If it doesn't, even better». You know that your world takes care of you and so if something has not worked out, it means that you have avoided other problems you cannot yet see. With this light-hearted mood, you can calmly go on a date with the destiny you are creating for yourself. From this moment onwards, whatever happens, remember, everything will be just as it should be!

Interpretation

A person's life is made up of a chain of cause and effect relationships, just like any other movement of matter. In the variants space, the effect is always located close to its cause. Just as one is derived from the other, so nearby sectors of the variants space come together in a lifeline. Every event on a lifeline has two branches, one leading in a favourable direction and the other in an unfavourable direction. Every time you face any kind of event in your life, you choose how to respond. If you think of the event as something positive, then you step onto the favourable branch of your lifeline. However, the tendency towards negativity forces you to express your discontent and choose the unfavourable branch. As soon as something makes you angry, another unpleasant situation follows. That is why 'troubles always come in threes'. The chain of bad luck, however, does not follow on from the first misfortune that occurred; it follows on from your relationship to that event. The pattern is created by the choice you make when you stand at the fork in the road. The coordination of intention principle equips you always to take the fortunate lifeline.

38. My World Cares

Principle

Make this a firm affirmation: «My world takes care of me». Whatever circumstances you encounter, even the most mundane, keep repeating this affirmation to yourself, whatever happens, good or bad. If you meet with a stroke of luck, do not forget to affirm that the world really is looking after you. State this affirmation in connection with every small detail. When you find circumstances disheartening, still affirm that everything is turning out as it should. Your world knows how to look after you much better than you do. How you look in the mirror is how things will be.

Interpretation

Adding gold to the mirror's reflective amalgam, as the Venetian masters used to do, makes everything in the reflection acquire warmer shades. Because the world is a mirror, you can tune it in the same way by creating your own amalgam. For example, you could choose, «My world takes care of me» as the dominant idea. Take it to be an axiom. Deliberately adjust your perception of the world to align with the dominant idea and then you will see how the mirror responds. Despite its simplicity, the amalgam technique is much more powerful than you might expect. If you have the patience to make this technique a habit, after some time you will be literally amazed at how much real influence your thoughts are having on your environment.

39. Against the Flow

Principle

Try to observe, at least for one day, how your mind paddles against the current. Someone offers you something and you turn it down. People try to tell you something but you dismiss it. Someone expresses their opinion and you argue with them. Someone is trying to do something in their own way but you direct them onto the true path. Someone offers you a solution but you object. You expect one thing but you get another and then express your discontent. Someone gets in your way and you are enraged. Something runs counter to your script and you launch a direct attack to get the flow back on track. Change your tactic. Shift the centre of gravity from control to observation. There is no point in thrashing your hands about in the water. Get out of your life's way. Let it go with the flow and you will be relieved to see just how much easier everything is.

Interpretation

The human mind works like a computer. It tries to calculate all its future moves and draw up a plan of action. The mind rarely manages to find the optimal approach to a situation, since the task involves too many unknowns, in addition to which, the situation is constantly changing as you go along. Yet still, it stubbornly insists on its own script, in other words, rows against the current. As a result, a huge amount of energy is wasted and the number of challenges and obstacles increases. The mind tries to control the flow itself, rather than how it moves with the flow. This is one of the main causes of the problems and issues people find themselves having to deal with. Rather than trying to be in control, try to observe more. Don't be too quick to dismiss, object, argue, insist, intervene, manage and criticise. Give the situation a chance to resolve itself before you actively intervene or resist. Let go of having to be in control and you will end up having more control over a situation than you had before. The only things worth controlling are your levels of inner and outer importance.

40. With the Variants Flow

Principle

Try to keep in balance with the outside world and trust the unfolding of the variants flow. Let go. Stop being the participant. Become the objective observer. Make it a rule that you always do things in the simplest way possible. When you have to solve a problem, ask yourself, «What is the simplest way of doing this?» If something does not go according to plan, let your grip go and accept the matter of an unforeseen alteration to your script. If someone offers you something, don't be too quick to refuse. If someone gives you a piece of advice, try mulling it over. When you hear a different opinion, don't be in too much of a hurry to enter into debate. If you think someone is going about something in the wrong way, let them. People take their own initiative. Allow them to realise their intentions. The variants flow is a sumptuous gift for the mind.

Interpretation

The mind is always busy developing its plan of further action. The mind is certain that it will weigh up everything and find the best possible way forward. Yet a plan already exists in the variants space. The information structure is arranged in a chain of cause and effect relationships. These relationships generate the variants flow, which arranges events simply and effectively. People are used to having to overcome obstacles and row against the current. Searching for complex solutions to simple problems becomes a habit. Nature does the opposite, always following the path of least resistance wasting no energy. For example, why does it often happen that after searching the entire region for a particular item you eventually find it right under your very nose? If you stay away from trouble and stop pushing against the variants flow, the solution will come of its own accord, and what is more, it will be the ideal solution.

41. The Habit of Remembering

Principle

In order to find a way out of a diffcult situation, you have to first recall that it originated as a consequence of amplified importance. A non-lucid dream, in which the events of the dream occur irrespective of your will, only has total control over you because you are unaware of the fact that you are dreaming. It is exactly the same in waking life. Until you become aware of the fact that you have allowed your mind to become totally immersed in a problem, circumstances will continue to control you. Stop. Shake off the delusion and remember that reality is a lucid dream, one you can control. Once you have woken up, practice Transurfing in your waking dream.

Interpretation

When you are floundering in inflated inner or outer importance, the most difficult thing is to return to awareness in the right moment. For this purpose, you need the Keeper, the inner observer, who keeps a constant eye on your level of awareness. Of course, it is hard to keep yourself in hand when you feel like going ballistic. Pendulums are like vampires. They use a kind of anesthesia i.e. your habit of falling asleep when you react negatively to an irritant. Even now, after having read these lines it may only be a matter of minutes before you get distracted, and take an unwanted phone call in an irritable tone of voice. Try to «wake up» several times during the day, look around you with a clear head, and understand that it is all a dream, and that you have been sleeping, not consciously aware of what you were doing. The habit of remembering is developed through consistent practice. Until being consciously aware becomes a habit, pendulums will do everything they can to get to you. Don't be dismayed. Overall, this will manifest itself as minor problems. Don't give in. Learn to remember and you will be victorious, you'll see.

42. Smashing Stereotypes

Principle

If someone tries to convince you that you must slave away for the benefit of someone or something, don't believe them. If they try to prove that nothing in this world is achieved except through hard work, don't listen to them. If someone tries to force you into a cruel battle for your place under the sun, don't listen to them. If someone tries to put you in your place, don't listen to them. If someone is trying to draw you into a sect or society which desperately needs your 'contribution to the common cause,' don't listen to them. If someone tries to tell you that you were born in poverty and therefore must live the rest of your life the same way, don't believe them. If someone insists that your options are limited, don't believe them.

Interpretation

From the point of view of common sense, everything in Transurfing is turned on its head. The same could be said of common sense from the point of view of Transurfing. If you do not want to live like everyone else, if you do not want to be content with middling achievements, if you aspire to live this one life to the fullest, then you are a Wanderer. In Transurfing, the Wanderer is not the one chosen by fate; fate is the one chosen by the Wanderer. Everything you want in life will be yours if you can tumble the monolith of common sense. People falsely assume that the rational worldview is an immutable law. It is not immutable but it is a 'thin' law and you can get around it. Unexplained 'miracles' happen more often than you would think. So why not let a miracle into your own life? All you have to do is give yourself permission to have what your soul desires. If you tear away the tangled web of prejudice and limitation, which pendulums

95

weave around you, and if you genuinely believe that you are worthy of your dreams and can give yourself permission to have the one thing you want with all your heart, then life will give it to you.

43. Visualising the Process

Principle

Whatever you do, your efficiency will be increased manifold, if rather than just doing it well, you consciously and enthusiastically admire your work, constantly asserting how excellent it is. This is extremely important! The principle here is this: «I do a wonderful job. Today, I am doing everything better than I did yesterday and tomorrow I will do it even better than today.» When you keep your goal slide in your mind, all your external circumstances will work towards achieving the goal, even if that does not appear to be the case. If you visualise the process as well, the layer of your personal world will rush towards your dream at lightning speed.

Interpretation

Let's say for example that you are working on some kind of project, creating something. Whilst you are working and afterwards, when you have finished for the day, imagine that the object of your creativity is becoming ever more perfect. Perhaps today, you added a few more details and tomorrow you will add several new touches. Imagine your creation becoming gradually transformed. You are constantly adding new elements to it watching it transform into a masterpiece before your very eyes. You are happy, enthralled by the creative process. Your brainchild grows with you. It is not just about contemplating your piece. You have to imagine the process of its birth and growth towards perfection. Create and marvel at the same time. Do not be shy to call yourself a genius. Affirm the thought form and ideas that are ever more brilliant will come to you. The same thing applies when you are working on your body. Nurture it as a mother nurtures her child. Imagine that your body is gradually acquiring perfect form. Look after it, train it and imagine your muscles developing, here and there becoming more toned. You will be surprised to find how efficiently the perfection affirmation is realised.

44. Slides

Principle

As a rule, people only take action within the limits of physical reality, guided by so-called common sense. This is not particularly effective. You now have a huge advantage. Once you start working with the metaphysical properties of reality, you can materialise whatever you intend. In order for a thought form to manifest in physical reality, you have to reproduce it systematically, running the goal slide through your mind, the picture of what your life would look like if you had already achieved your goal. Unlike useless dreaming that only occasionally comes into being, this is real work. Do the work and you will see the results.

Interpretation

When you practice the visualisation technique, the layer of your world shifts in the variants space to the sector in which your goal has been achieved. Do not think about how this happens. Your thoughts should be focused exclusively on the goal slide. In its own time, outer intention will open doors, real opportunities, the likes of which, you could never have foreseen and would not have appeared if you had not worked with the slide. When you see that the goal is getting closer, your fears and doubts will vanish. Do not watch the slide from the outside, like a film in the cinema. Live it, at least virtually. Pretend it is already happening. Imagine all sorts of new details. Don't let working with the slide become a burden or chore. Just take pleasure in envisioning the scene in which you have already achieved your goal. Of course, if your visualisation is not very distinct, do not try too hard to make it clearer. Work on everything in your own way, however it comes. Most importantly, if you work on your slide systematically and enthusiastically, you can consider your goal already in the bag.

45. Path to Your Goal

Principle

Drop the importance of your goal, let go of any feelings of longing so that all you are left with is the resolve to have. You should be moving towards your goal in the same way that you go to the postbox to pick up your post. The only things that can spoil everything on the path towards your goal are obsessional commitment, trying too hard and fear of defeat. Run the goal slide in your mind without including any particular script. You already have it. Don't think about the means of achieving the goal. If you focus on the goal as if you had already achieved it, after some time, outer intention will open the door of opportunity to you, and then the means to the end will present themselves.

Interpretation

If you think your goal is unachievable, you will spoil the whole thing with doubt and heavy thoughts about your own potential failure. So how do you believe in the impossible enough for it to become possible? You don't! There is no way that you can persuade, convince, or force yourself to believe. Put these petty worries to one side and get down to it. Run the goal slide in your thoughts and do not forget to put one foot in front of the other as you move towards your goal. Don't worry that for now, your goal is hidden from view somewhere way beyond the clouds. Of course, it is difficult for you to imagine how it could be yours but that is not for you to worry about. All you have to do is make your order. Leave the rest to the waiter. When the mind sees the doors opening, your doubts will dissolve. Many people, who have achieved astounding success, confess that they would never have believed themselves capable of it. Just one piece of advice: Don't place Your entire goal on one card only. Find an alternative route, a safety net or fall-back position; don't slam past doors shut and don't burn your bridges prematurely.

46. Doors

Principle

Your door is the path that will lead you to your goal. Keep running your goal slide through your mind and, sooner or later, outer intention will reveal opportunities to you i.e. your doors. If you get tired, suffer huge energy loss and exhaust yourself on the path to your goal, you've gone through a door that isn't yours. I am not saying that it will be easy but if you feel spiritually uplifted and inspired then you can be sure that what you are doing is your door. Everything that you do easily, gracefully and with enthusiasm will have meaning and value. Any small thing you do that is characteristic of your personality, even if it is totally valueless in the context of set stereotypes, could be the key to your door. Try projecting your characteristic, 'frivolous' child-like quality onto grown up doors.

Interpretation

Pendulums have taught people to do what they have to and to accept their lot. People become so accustomed to what has to be done that the true inclinations of their soul are pushed away into the furthest corners of their conscious mind for better times ahead. But life comes to an end and the better times never come. Happiness always looms somewhere in the future. The false stereotype asserts that if this future is to be your present, it has to be fought for, earned and finally achieved. People often stop doing what they love for financial reasons. Their activities are divided into hobbies and the real work, which gives them an income. In reality, you can earn money from a hobby if that is your goal. In this world, everything that is done with soul, is very expensive. Yet the false stereotype of forced necessity prevents people from completely devoting themselves to their goal. They will slog their guts out for some other geezer for most of their life because it is supposedly, what they have to do to exist. The soul gets a few crumbs left over after the main working day. So for whom does a person live? For some old geezer?

47. Co-dependent Relationships

Principle

If you think that the world is against you, think: to what object or item do you attach excessively important significance? If you attract everything you hate, if you are haunted by everything that irritates you, and if everything that is most undesirable happens to you after all, then it is because you are gripping the world by the throat and it is resisting, trying to break free. The more you insist on your own desires and claims, the stronger the magnet that attracts the opposite. Relax your grip. Let the world do whatever it likes. Give yourself permission to be yourself and allow others to be different. Don't compare yourself to anyone. Don't get too attached to anything. Accept things with grace and let them go with grace.

Interpretation

When any quality is attributed excessive importance, excess potential is created, which distorts the surrounding energetic environment. Excess potential is not necessarily a problem, as long as the distorted evaluation exists relative only to itself. As soon as the artificially inflated value of one object is positioned in comparative relationship to another, polarisation arises which functions as a magnet for trouble. Dependent relationships are created between people when they start comparing themselves to one another, compartmentalising and placing conditions like: «If you are this, then I am that». This is why trouble creeps into our lives so intrusively, as if on purpose. You can see for example, how totally incompatible individuals marry as if they were trying to punish one other. In any team, there will always be that one person you find particularly irritating. Murphy's law or what we would call 'sod's law' is the same principle at work. All conflict is based on comparison and opposition. Draw your own conclusions.

48. The Search for Love

Principle

There is no need to go searching for love. Love will find you. To meet your other half, systematically run a slide in which you imagine your life together with some abstract individual who represents your ideal. At a certain point, a door will open and he or she will appear. From then on it will be up to you. You have to go through the door, take the first step, letting go of blind pride and any sort of prejudice. Take this step simply and sincerely without masquerade or affectation. Unaffectedness is always compelling. Likewise, always be yourself. Don't try and change who you really are under any circumstances. Stay true to your own credo. Then the dual mirror will stay free of crooked distortion.

Interpretation

A romantic slide should contain an abstract person who represents your ideal. You should only include a person you already know in your slide in the extreme case that no other means of finding requited love is open to you. In principle, you can run a slide in which you are both together and love each other. This is a script of a kind and so consequently, it will exist in the variants space but the other person concerned is not a passive object. They are a living being who is also actively realising their intention. You might have some success with the slide but it won't be very effective because no living person is stationary in the variants space. They are always hurrying about. Whilst you are busy 'sliding' the other person will quickly find for themselves a more 'grounded' partner. What's more, the soul of the person who is being 'slided' will feel it happening and if they don't like it, they may subconsciously begin to experience a feeling of aversion towards you. The best way of going about things is not to take the risk at all and arm yourself with the Frailing principle. Interpersonal relationships are the one case when you are forced to communicate with another living being rather than hanging about dreaming with your head in the clouds.

49. Extinguishing a Pendulum

Principle

Be prepared for the pendulums to provoke you. When you find yourself in an unpleasant situation or when you receive bad news, you are naturally thrown off balance. In the standard scenario, you ought to worry, be afraid, run away, lose heart or express your dissatisfaction or irritation. Now, do the opposite. Offer an abnormal response. Smash the script and try substitution: replace fear with confidence, despondency with enthusiasm, indignation with indifference and irritation with joy. The essence of the pendulum game is to pull you off balance. You have to break the rules of the game intentionally. Do whatever you like, just as long as it is not what people expect and then, victory will be yours.

Interpretation

Pendulums feed on human energy. For example, when something makes you angry, you express your fury and give your energy away to the pendulum. The pendulums provoke everything, which could potentially evoke strong, negative emotions. When you come across some unfortunate circumstance and react by getting irritated, there is a continuation and the negative situation develops in the same spirit, or new unpleasant situations arise. That is how the pendulum swings. You swing the pendulum yourself when you accept the game imposed on you. Behave differently. Either don't react at all or respond in the opposite way altogether and then you will still the pendulum's sway. Your task is to introduce a different game, your own game, by reacting in an abnormal manner. The sole principle here lies in the fact that when you swing with a different frequency to the resonant frequency, a dissonance is set up between you and the pendulum which causes the pendulum to stop swinging in relationship to your energy, as a result of which, it will leave you alone.

50. The Pendulum Flop

Principle

If you let thoughts of what you don't like bug you, this is what will show up in your life. In order to let go of what you don't want, you have to accept it first. By 'accept', I don't mean 'let it in' so much as 'acknowledge its right to exist and then pass by indifferently'. Accept and let go. In other words, consider the fact of it and then wave goodbye. At the pendulum's first attack always respond by agreeing and then either diplomatically step back or unobtrusively direct the pendulum's momentum in a direction that suits you. Learn 'not to get hooked' and to ignore the things that irritate you and they will disappear from your world. When the pendulum has no way of hooking into you, it disappears into the void.

Interpretation

Pendulums are the lords of dreams. When a person is susceptible to their provocation, it is as if they fall asleep because being wholly immersed in the imposed game, their mind is zombified by what is happening. If something irritates you or evokes a sharp sense of aversion, you might as well be walking around with a hook in your head. Catching onto your hook, the pendulum will instantly set about finding a suitable irritant, and not just one. You will dangle from the hook for as long as your irritation has «no end». In order to pull the hook out of your mind, you have to change your relationship towards the irritant and divert its attention, accept the situation, transform the tragedy into a comedy and focus on doing something else. Changing your relationship to something does not mean bottling up your emotions. Emotions stuffed deep inside are the very 'evil' which builds up and then inevitably explodes and goes to feed the pendulums. First, express your emotions and then consciously correct your relationship. There is no point in fighting a pendulum. They simply have to be ignored.

51. Incomprehensible Infinity

Principle

Why does Transurfing work? Who 'put' everything into the variants space? No one 'created' the variants space. It has always existed. It is human nature to believe that everything in this world was made by someone or something and has a tangible beginning and end. Yet there are certain questions in this world to which the answers lie way beyond the limits of the human mind, for the mind is nothing more than a logic machine, albeit a machine with the ability for abstract thought. Transurfing does not explain the structure of the world; it offers a utilitarian model that enables us to understand why it is possible for a person to create their own reality and how to go about it.

It's the same as driving a car without understanding how it was assembled.

Interpretation

All scientists have ever tried to do throughout human history is explain how the world works. This process will continue for eternity. Every existing model will be replaced by ever-newer versions of how the world works. If you stand in front of one mirror while holding another mirror you will understand how it is that there can be an infinite number of models, which explain how the universe works. When one manifestation of reality is taken as the foundation for a model, what you get is a separate version, a small piece of the mirror. When you stand in front of the main mirror of the world holding that smaller piece, you see a new facet of the world reflected. When you take one of the manifestations of this aspect, you again get a separate reflection of reality. And again, out of yet another tiny mirror, a new one will appear, reflected in the image of the mirror before that. So what is the true nature of the world? Try (if you can) to imagine it as being as two identical mirrors placed just opposite each other. Both mirrors reflect the image of the mirror placed in front of them. In both mirrors, nothing is reflected an infinite number of times. This is the black infinity of images where nothing is a reflection of nothing. Are any of the concepts available to the rational mind adequate to describe this scene? Hardly.

52. **Gatekeeper to Eternity**

Principle

The variants space contains everything, and everything that you desire with your heart and mind is yours. You should know, however, that at the threshold of Eternity there stands a Gatekeeper, an absolute law, which guards access to everything beyond. The unremitting guardian only admits those who have the audacity to exercise the right of the Master. Your pass is the verdict: «I am capable and worthy because I have decided it is so. I don't want and I don't hope. I intend.» Claim this right and the Gatekeeper will throw open the gates to eternity.

Interpretation

What makes a showbiz star different to the girl next door, a luminary of science different to the timid student and the chosen ones different from the rank and file? The answer is 'one single step'. There are those who have been bold enough to claim their right and there are others who are still procrastinating and do not believe that they are capable or worthy. The firm conviction holds in the minds of the timid that the chosen ones exist because all the rest have chosen them on account of their having some exceptionally outstanding quality. In reality, this is a false stereotype. The chosen ones choose themselves. It is only after taking this step and because of it that others notice them. Claim the right to be a chosen one. Say to yourself: «From this moment on, I choose myself». It is not that you have the right because you are worthy and capable. You have it, the right, as a matter of course. The variants space contains everything including something that is intended for you personally — your verdict that you have this right. This is your pass to Eternity. It sanctions the privilege to create your own reality.

53. Shaping Your Own Destiny

Principle

When a person takes control into their own hands, their life is no longer dependent on circumstances. The little ship of life can be steered in any direction away from the 'fate' that is allegedly predetermined for you. It is all very simple. Life is like a river. If you row the boat yourself, you can choose which direction in which you want to travel. If you simply give yourself up to the current, you will have no choice but to float in the direction the current carries you. If you want karma, you will have karma. When you think that your fate depends on some set of unforgiving circumstances or the mistakes of past lives, you bring that corresponding variant of your potential future into physical reality. The will is yours, for you are the child of God. If you want to be a Master, then this too is in your power. The dual mirror will agree to anything.

Interpretation

Suppose someone sets a goal, which from a normal point of view seems difficult to achieve or totally impossible. The person strives towards their goal with all their heart but the sceptical mind drops it and keeps asking the same old question: «But how?» In accordance with the principles of Transurfing, at a stage when the means of achieving a goal are not yet clear, one has to take the unconventional step of forgetting about the means and concentrating on the end goal, as if it were already achieved. When you roll the goal slide in your mind, the layer of your personal world shifts in the variants space to the sector in which the goal is realised. The shift is subtle but real. Your mind can doubt as much as it wants. All that matters is that it diligently runs the mental picture of your goal slide. It is like being on a nighttime flight. You can barely tell that the plane is moving, but the engine is working so you know it must be moving. In the same way, the mind runs the visualisation of your goal (the engine), while outside the lifting force, outer intention, pulls the layer of your world (the airplane) towards its destination. The boat wheel of intention is in your hands. Everything will turn out the way you want it to.

54. Spiritual Laziness

Principle

When a person believes in a prediction of their fate or takes a dream very seriously, they unwittingly create a thought form, which can be manifested as a program. Realisation only occurs because the person believes in all that nonsense. We always get what we believe in. But it is childishly silly and naive to turn to any old man or woman who is supposedly capable of predicting the future rather than creating your own destiny at your own discretion. You are the true Master of your fate if you intend it to be so. Do not sacrifice your fate to the mirror makers!

Interpretation

Only the infantile believe in horoscopes, those for whom life is like a non-lucid dream. If you intend to shape your own destiny, there will be no point in enlisting the services of a mirror maker. For who are astrologers, interpreters, and predictors if not mirror makers? After all, they are not just offering harmless forecasts but a surrogate part of your destiny, a piece of the mirror into which you will have to peer. You receive a kind of affirmation of the future, which sits in your subconscious mind programming how your fate will unfold. Money aside, do you really think that you can get a piece of the future just like that? Peering into the Book of fate is not without its consequences. And the payment for this product is always the same: you take it with you and integrate it into your life, whether you want to or not. Showing interest in a forecast is like being given a mirror and asking the mirror maker whether or not you may smile in it. Yet, you already have a mirror - the layer of your world, from which you can create anything you like. With your own mirror, you are free. Whenever you wish, you can use the will of the Master to transform defeat into victory, and that is how it will be. Who gives a damn about predictions?

55. The Master's Mindset

Principle

People paint the layer of their personal world in the darkest shades with their own negative attitude. The mirror simply states the content of the attitude and ignores your slant on it. It does not matter how you are thinking about something. What matters is what you are thinking about in the first place. Whether you like the reflection or not, you are still thinking about it. Only the theme of your thoughts has weight. From this moment on, make it a rule to keep your thought pattern and mindset under control. Whatever happens, turn everything into a positive. Fix your attention ultimately on what you want to have. With time, you will create a very comfortable personal reality. Prepare yourself for a magnificent cascade of pleasing events.

Interpretation

Usually, a person's attention is totally absorbed by their negative experiences. They become preoccupied with the things they don't like. They think about the things they don't want and don't want the things they think about. The mirror makes no allowances for a person's desires or reluctance. It simply accurately conveys the content of the image, no more, no less. It is ridiculous really. People are endlessly dragging around with them the things they do not like. That is why the poor get poorer and the rich get richer. They are all looking in the mirror of the world each in their own way stating the guise of their personal reality. This kind of reality sucks you in like a swamp. The old woman queuing for her pension, the exhausted woman with heavy bags on a packed bus, and the sick patient hoboing from one medical institution to the next - all their thoughts totally immersed in their own grim reality. Meanwhile, someone else is enjoying life, the ocean, yachts, travel, luxury hotels, and expensive restaurants, everything the heart desires. In every case, irrespective of the nature of the situation, people make precisely the same statement: «Such is life». More precisely, our life is as we imagine our existence to be. The mirror confirms and consistently consolidates the content of our thought forms.

56. Dissatisfaction with the World

Principle

If you really want to improve your life, replace re-active negativity with a positive dominant, for example, «My world always chooses the best for me. I go with the variants flow and the world meets me half way. I create the layer of my world with my own intention. My world protects me. My world guards me against problems. My world makes sure that my life is easy and comfortable. I place an order and my world delivers it. I may not know how to take care of me but my world does. My intention is manifesting in physical reality. Everything is leading towards it and everything is as it should be.» Remember, either you control reality or reality controls you.

Interpretation

Why is it that with time, all life's colours fade, and quiet serenity is replaced with anxious concerns? Is this because the number of problems we face increases with age? No, it's because as a person matures, they tend to adopt a more negative attitude. Discontent is a more powerful emotion than the feeling of satisfaction that comes from comfort and tranquility. Despite everything, not realising that they are happy in this moment, people demand more and more of life. The little poppet's demands grow and the child becomes more spoiled and ungrateful. Naturally, the world cannot keep up with the brat's rapidly growing demands and the darling poppet starts to express its grievances changing its attitude towards the world: «You're bad! You don't give me what I want! You don't care about me!» The full force of the unity of discontented soul and unhappy mind buys into the negative attitude completely. Meanwhile, the world is just a mirror and has no choice but to throw up its hands sadly and reply, «As you wish little sparrow. Have it your way». As a result of this dynamic, reality, the reflection of a person's thoughts, changes for the worse.

57. Inferiority

Principle

When a person begins to realise that they don't fit conventional standards, they begin to feel inadequate but in comparison to whom? Ask yourself, do you want to be like everyone else, or do you want to be yourself? You won't succeed in being yourself if you try to hide your shortcomings. You will start to feel like you are being yourself if you focus on developing your finer qualities. Any inferiority you feel will be balanced out by your inherent merits. Charm can compensate for a lack of beauty. Self-confidence can compensate for physical defects. The ability to listen can replace the inability to speak freely. There is just one piece of advice I would give to anyone who suffers from being shy: Guard this quality for the treasure that it really is. Shyness will always have a certain mysterious charm, as long as you don't play it up into the luxury of being 'too cool'.

Interpretation

Feelings of inferiority are based on comparison: "I'm not only unattractive outwardly; I have no talents or particular ability. I'm not intelligent or witty and I don't know how to communicate with people. I'm not worth anything... No, it's much more serious than that. The fact is that I'm less than they are!" This type of thinking is an example of a dependent relationship in its purest form. It creates polarisation: «They are good, I am bad». Polarisation generates the wind of balancing forces, which cause a person to try and raise their artificially understated value in any way possible. Therefore, the person begins to behave unnaturally emphasising even more, the aspects of self they are trying to hide. Battling with an inferiority complex can create far more unpleasant consequences than the complex itself. There is only one way to eliminate a complex like this. Stop comparing yourself to others and switch the focus of your attention from your shortcomings to your strengths. Create a positive slide in which your strengths are in such full bloom that your shortcomings fade into the background. Live in this virtual slide and soon it will be transformed into reality.

58. Self-sufficiency

Principle

The fact remains that you have colossal potential even if you cannot see it. You are capable of doing anything; it is just that no one has told you that yet. Accept as a fundamental truth the fact that your soul can do anything and then give yourself permission to make the most of it. Stop looking for truth in sources outside yourself. Take a good look inside and there you will find the answers to all your questions. 'Looking inside' is not an abstraction. Simply ask yourself a question and dare to answer it yourself. By connecting to the corresponding sector in the variants space, you are quite capable of making a discovery, building something new or creating a masterpiece. Stop looking at established authorities. They turned to the same source in their own time. Now it is your turn.

Interpretation

Do you enjoy the works of geniuses of art, science, business, sport, variety, and cinema? You can become one of them. The reason you enjoy works of a genius is that they are born of the soul. Others will enjoy your creation also, but only if it originates in your unique soul. Everything mediocre and ordinary is created by the mind. Creations of the mind, like the mind itself, are never unique. Only your soul is unique. You possess a real treasure. Any brilliant creation you produce can only be born from your soul. Let your mind allow she to create. You just have to stop being distracted by other people's experience and stereotypical standards. Create your own. When faced with literally any kind of problem, shape the question and give yourself time to find the answer. You will see, the answer will come of itself (it already exists in the variants space). Your task is to hold the intention of coming up with it on your own. There is just one requirement: in order to 'attune yourself' to the necessary sector in the variants space, you have to have certain basic skills and knowledge in that area. Beyond that, just be very attentive to the voice of your heart, which is trying to communicate with you in the language of intuition.

59. Decision Making

Principle

When you consider how to act in any given situation, only your mind is working. It analyses the advantages and disadvantages, builds a concept that is sound and persuasive and, at the same time, takes account of the opinions of others. As a rule, it does not take into account the premonitions of the heart. In this regard, the mind might as well be fast asleep. So, let it sleep and don't bother it until it has come to a decision. Once the decision is made stop listening to anyone else. Wake up and scrutinise how you felt when you made the decision. How comfortable your soul feels in this moment will reveal the heart's response to the mind's decision.

Interpretation

Every time you have to make a decision, listen first to the voice of reason and then listen to the feeling in your soul. As soon as the mind has made a decision, the soul will respond either positively or negatively. In the case of the latter, you will experience a small wave of something, a sneaking suspicion in your soul. When you made the decision, you will have experienced the briefest inkling of something. At that moment though, the mind will have been so absorbed in its analysis that it would not have bothered about your feelings. Now though, remember. What was that initial fleeting feeling? If it was a sinking feeling on the background of optimistic reasoning, the soul clearly said, «No». If your soul is saying, 'no' and your mind is saying, 'yes' boldly refuse if you can. The soul always knows exactly what she wants. There is one simple, reliable algorithm for determining a heartfelt 'no'. If you have to convince yourself and persuade yourself to say yes, then the soul is really saying no. Remember, when your soul does say 'yes' to something you won't have to persuade yourself.

60. The Rustle of the Morning Stars

Principle

When you are faced with a problem and don't know exactly what the solution is, trust your intuition. If you rely on premonitions, you are bound to make mistakes but you will make infinitely more mistakes by only heeding the voice of reason. When you have to make a decision, no one knows what to do better than your soul. It can often be very difficult to understand what exactly your soul is trying to tell you but you can tell unambiguously whether your soul approves of the mind's decision or not. That wave of uneasiness you feel in response to a decision made by the rational mind is a reliable criterion for the truth.

Interpretation

The mind thinks with the help of well-established signs: symbols, words, concepts, diagrams, rules, and so on. The soul does not use these categories. She does not think or speak, she feels and knows. Moreover, the mind is constantly busy with its own chatter. It believes that everything can be rationally explained and saved. When the mind slackens off, intuitive feelings and knowledge can break through into consciousness. The mind gets distracted and in this moment, you sense the feelings and knowledge that are the realm of the soul. This is the rustling of the morning stars, the voice of no words, reflection without thinking, and sound without volume. You understand something but only vaguely. You do not argue, you feel intuitively. You simply know. The soul has access to the information field and can find the answers to many questions as well as protect you from taking erroneous or even dangerous steps if you just listen to her voice. For example, if you feel a certain uncharacteristic anxiety before boarding a plane, it would be wise not to board the flight. Likewise, when you fiirst meet someone of the opposite sex and you have to persuade yourself that he (she) is right for you, it is highly likely that any further relationship will not last.

61. Borrowed Goals

Principle

When you are deciding on your own goal, ask yourself, "Do I really want this with all my soul or do I just want to want it?" If you have to convince yourself then it is a borrowed goal. If the goal is truly yours, you won't have to sell it to yourself. The movement towards borrowed goals always holds the joy in an illusory future. When you are moving towards your own goal, you are happy in the moment. Borrowed goals are always brutal to the self, a compulsion, an obligation. A borrowed goal always takes the guise of fashion and prestige, seduces with its superiority and forces you to prove yourself to everyone. Borrowed goals are imposed on you by others and serve only to improve someone else's welfare. Seek your own goal.

Interpretation

Borrowed goals evoke that uneasy feeling in the soul. False goals tend to be very attractive. Your mind will paint the positive values of the goal in the brightest of colours and yet if you feel in any way burdened by the goal, despite its attractiveness, it is paramount that you be honest with yourself. Naturally, the mind does not want to know. As far as it is concerned, everything is wonderful and perfect. So where does the sombre shade come from? When considering your goal, forget about its potential prestige, how difficult it is to achieve or even how to achieve it. Focus your attention solely on the sense you have in your core. Imagine that you have already achieved your goal and everything is behind you. Do you feel good or not? Don't confuse the inhibitions of the scared ego (or shyness thinking, 'Could this really be for me?') with an uneasy gut reaction. Those sneaky suspicions are actually a heavy feeling of oppression or burden, which you are vaguely beginning to sense lurking beyond the optimistic reasoning of the mind. Slides can help overcome spiritual inhibition but spiritual discomfort... never.

62. Your Personal Goal

Principle

Every human being carries a precious treasure inside, the unique quality of the soul. Every soul has its own goal and when a person is on the path to their personal goal, they find true happiness. Happiness is not somewhere ahead of you in the future. Either you have it here and now or you do not have it at all. The secret of true success is to free yourself from pendulums and choose your own path. Ask yourself this question: «What is your soul's passion? What would turn your life into an ongoing celebration?» Don't think about restrictions or limitations. Don't hold back. Indulge,

123

order whatever you want. If the goal is yours, the soul will sing when you think about it and the mind will rub its hands with glee.

Interpretation

The human soul can only vaguely guess what she wants. The mind has to help her choose her goal. But the mind tries, in its usual manner, to find the goal by means of logic. That is a mistake. The mind's task is not to search for the goal but to recognise it in time. In the right place at the right time, the soul will divine its own goal and then you will know. The main thing is to give the soul the chance to meet its goal. You have to expand your horizons, visit places you have never been before, watch things you have never seen before, allow new information in and break the mundane cycle of everyday life. Beyond that, stay aware and attentive to the voice of the heart. Give yourself an indefinite window of time. Do not force yourself into fixed timelines and don't turn searching for your goal into a chore. Simply hold this thought: «I am looking for the thing that will turn my life into a constant celebration». The goal will come as a revelation. When you come across information that lights your soul up and your mind takes great pleasure in pondering it from all sides, and then you can assume that you have found the very thing.

63. The Boat Wheel of Intention

Principle

If you want to achieve your goal, you have to turn desire into firm intention. Dreams don't come true. Stop longing for your goal. If you hold the intention, it is already yours. Longing is the fear of failure: "I want it so much but I don't have the energy and at the same time, I'm afraid it won't work out." Why are you afraid? Because you are not thinking about the goal so much as how to achieve it. Stop thinking about the how. Your task is to think about your goal as a fait accompli and run this goal slide in your mind. On the path to your goal, things won't go as you expect or it might be that nothing happens at all. Don't let that discourage you. No matter how events unfold, keep your course in a direct line with your goal. Let this be your motto: «I don't want and I don't hope, I intend».

Interpretation

Your position in the variants space relative to your goal is as if you were in a boat on the open sea. In order to reach land, you have to sail in a northerly direction. The direction in which the compass needle is pointing represents the focus of your train of thought. All the time that you envisage a mental picture of approaching the shore and stepping out onto dry land, your 'needle' will point where it should. All you have to do is paddle and concentrate on arriving, just this and nothing else. Then the impatient mind begins to fidget and bother the rower: «Are we heading in the right direction? Will we be much longer?What if you do not have the strength? What if we're going in the wrong direction? Of course! We should be going in the opposite direction entirely!» As a result, the compass needle begins to waver and the boat constantly shifts its course. The mind doubts and worries because it cannot perceive movement in the variants space. It is used to having the situation under control. The mind will only calm down if you give it a task so that it can understand what it is doing. So tell your mind not to rock the boat and to keep the wheel firmly fixed on course. Controlling your train of thought, that is what the mind should be working on.

64. The Soul's Sail

Principle

Everyone has their own personal goal, on the path to which, they reveal all their talents and find true happiness. If a person is unaware of their uniqueness, their divine power from the Creator, and falls into non-lucid dreaming, the pendulums will put the dreamer into instant circulation, impose false goals and show them their place in the matrix, so that they become nothing more than a cog in the system. When a person aims for borrowed goals, their life can feel as if they were serving a prison sentence. On the path towards your personal goal, you will find true happiness in life. Your goal will transform your life into a constant celebration. Achieving your goal will bring with it the fulfilment of all your other desires, and what is more, the results will surpass your highest expectations. Search for your goal and you will find it.

Interpretation

Is it really necessary to search for a personal goal? In truth, most people don't even think about it. They just live their life and that's it, although they are not so much living it as serving time. One day is very much like another: routine work, the same old faces, streets, walls, the ropey range of distractions, the permanent burden of cares and responsibilities, and celebrations only on certain days (although not chosen by you). Yet there are other people, whose lives are always bright and colourful like a carnival. For these lucky ones, there are not any workdays as such. 'At work they work' as if they were playing and every day is a Catherine wheel of interesting events, happy experiences, and meetings. «Why is it like that for them but not for me?» Because these chosen ones sought their own path. You can count these kinds of people on the fingers of one hand. The rest are prisoners of the matrix, rank-and-file components of the system. Unaware that they are renouncing their right to freedom of choice in the process, God's uniquely powerful children have allowed pendulums to turn their lives into a non-lucid dream. Now the system decides for them what they need and want, how they should live their life and what they should strive for.

127

65. Pessimism

Principle

When a person looks at their reflection in the mirror and sees traits they don't like, they focus their attention on them and express their negative relationship towards them in an automatic response. As a result, everything becomes worse than it was previously. The mirror reflection of reality slowly darkens and pales together with the thought form. Their world loses its former freshness of colour and becomes increasingly bleak and miserable. Stop picking at the things that irritate you and they will cease to annoy you. Stop looking for problems. Search for solutions. Finally, stop whining. Once you have changed your relationship to life, you will start to experience the solid feeling that everything is unfolding as it should and that things can only get better. Everything will turn out as it should.

Interpretation

The tendency to express pessimistic expectations is quite unattractive to others. The attitude of 'there's no point; nothing will come of it anyway' is a form of sadomasochism. The pessimist derives a perverse satisfaction from wallowing in their sorry lot: "Everything is so bad, it simply couldn't get any worse. It serves them right and me too!" The loser tends to state their unenviable position with the same fatal doom, «Life is totally dark and there's no light at the end of the tunnel.» People with this kind of attitude dislike their fate so much that they put all their mental energy into complaining about it and lamenting their lot. Yet what else can the mirror possibly reflect if the image opposite it expresses nothing but discontent. As the image, "I am unhappy, I don't want this!", so the reflection: "Yes, you are unhappy, and no, you don't want this". The mirror reflects the fact, nothing more, nothing less. And because this is so, the number of reasons to be dissatisfied with life increases which in turn worsens that person's relationship to the world. Therefore, the former favourite transforms into a mere grouch, deprived by their own fate and constantly complaining about how much the world owes them. It is sad to see it. People don't understand that they spoil things themselves.

66. Support

Principle

If things are hard for you at the moment, you can always find support inside yourself if you wake up and look at how your problem arose in the first place. The danger lies not in the problem itself but in your relationship to it. Immersing yourself in the importance of the problem, you give your energy to the pendulum. You have to realise that in any problematic situation the pendulum will want you either to prepare yourself for a fight or throw in the towel and give in to despondency. You must not do either. So if you have no support and you've lost your iron rod of confidence, what can you do? Confidence will come when you wake up and acknowledge how the game is played. You will chuckle wryly to yourself, «Ah, it's you, a pendulum?» You won't hook me that easily, not this time!» You are no longer a puppet. You are free.

Interpretation

The world can start to look intimidating and hostile to a person who is not familiar with the rules of the game. Surging feelings of loneliness and depression can cause a person to fall asleep and give in to the will of circumstance. When faced with a complex problem or unfortunate news, people give their energy to the pendulum and then they feel anxious, lacking in energy and burdened by the pressure of the whole situation. Either they shift into a state of readiness for combat or they just feel hopeless and give up. Both states are abnormal and lead to stress and depression. In order to find support, people chase the situation down by smoking cigarettes and drugs, drinking alcohol and turning to other similar kinds of emotional prop. As a result, they get caught in bondage to other pendulums. All you have to do is wake up and observe the game as a member of the audience would only without exiting the stage. You will be able to see all the hidden rocks lying on the seabed as easily as if the sea had suddenly evaporated. Then you will be able to come to a position of strength inside yourself. Understanding what is happening around you counts for a lot. Only this knowledge is enough to restore a quiet, firm belief in oneself, for lack of confidence usually results from fear of the unknown. Knowing all this, you can now turn your life into a clear waking dream and gain control over any situation in which you find yourself.

67. Refining the Script

Principle

Look at everything around you with the eyes of an observer. Imagine that you are taking part in a play at the same time acting dispassionately taking note of any movement in your surroundings. Do not insist on keeping to your own script. Let the world go with the variants flow. This does not mean that you have to agree with everything totally. It is one thing to close your eyes and surrender to the powerful pull of the current, and quite another to go with the flow, deliberately and consciously. You will know when to pull in the reins and when to give some slack. Let the world go and observe its movement. Keep an eye on it, like a wise mentor who leaves the youth room for freedom of choice only occasionally giving a nudge in the right direction. You will soon notice how the world begins to centre around you.

Interpretation

People feel uncomfortable when they are lead blindfolded. The mind finds it difficult to accept that sometimes nothing happens or that events don't turn out as planned. The mind is designed like a cybernetic automaton. If the work algorithm is broken, a red light comes on. So-called common sense can really be very primitive. It not only sets a stereotypical course of action, it also insists upon it being carried out. In the majority of cases, there is no need to take action and it is quite enough to be flexible and gently follow what is happening. As long as you don't disturb it, the variants flow will direct the course of events down a preferable stream. You have to turn the shortsighted intention of the mind in the opposite direction. Let it dynamically adjust its script to include the unexpected. This kind of task will be new to the mind, but it is the only effective way of shedding the role of the kitten playing in front of a mirror. When you consciously abandon control of a situation, you end up gaining real control instead.

68. Box for the Soul

Principle

Your soul did not come into the material world in order to suffer. Yet it is of benefit to the pendulums that the battle for a place in the sun is the norm. Your soul came into the world as if to a celebration. Give yourself permission to see life in that way. Only you can decide whether you spend your entire life working for the benefit of a foreign pendulum or living for yourself, for your own pleasure. If you choose the celebration, then you need to break free from the pendulums that restrain you and find your personal goal and your personal door. Unite your mind and heart and you will have anything your heart desires, literally and figuratively. Allow yourself the luxury of being worthy of the best.

Interpretation

We cannot change the world and so we have to learn to accept the things that do not depend on us. Many limitations and conventions literally lock the soul up in a box. Captured by pendulums, the mind becomes the soul's jailer preventing it from realising its potential. A person is forced to behave as the world of pendulums wants them to, expressing dissatisfaction, getting irritated, competing and fighting. Be aware that this is simply the pendulum's game. The reason it is a game and not a battle is that essentially, pendulums are like clay dummies. In the game, your potential is only limited by intention. The level of importance your attribute to things and your own level of awareness can limit the pendulum's potential. When importance and attachment are at zero, the pendulums will fall through your emptiness. You will draw strength from the realisation that you understand the rules of the game. As soon as you notice a pendulum trying to hook you and pull you off balance, smile to yourself, and assertively drop your importance levels. Then you will feel your strength and understand that you can decide the game script. When you win the pendulum's game, you acquire freedom of choice.

69. Idealisation

Principle

When a person creates their own myths, sooner or later they are always dispelled. If you don't want to experience disappointment, observe the 'three don't's rule'. Whatever happens, don't increase your levels of attributed importance. Nothing is quite as important as it would wish to appear. Don't make an idol of anyone. They are much more earth-bound than they look. Don't sugarcoat reality. Everything is really quite prosaic. Strive always to evaluate reality in a sober manner.

Interpretation

When you think that there is something somewhere, which does not actually exist, excess potential appears creating a distortion in the surrounding energy field. Balancing forces try to eliminate the heterogeneity and, in the majority of cases, their action is aimed at 'debunking the myth'. For example, a young, romantic, dreamy lad imagines the object of his love to be an 'angel of pure beauty'. In reality, it turns out that she is a very down-to-earth young lady, who loves her fun and is not remotely inclined to share the tragic dreaming of the starry-eyed youth. Or, a woman paints a mental portrait of her ideal husband. The firmer her belief that he should be exactly as she has pictured him, the more powerful the excess potential that is created.

Only a character with completely the opposite qualities can discharge it. And vice versa, if a woman really detests drunkenness and rudeness, she will fall into the trap of finding someone who is an alcoholic or an outright yob. People attract the things they actively dislike and vice versa, if they begin to idealise something excessively, balancing forces will force them to face a harsh reality.

70. Unconditional Love

Principle

If someone has fallen in love with you, consider it a miracle. Even if the feeling is not mutual, don't cold-shoulder it. Treat the love shown to you with high regard and treat it very gently. If you think about it, being loved is a miracle. What if this is the last person who will ever fall in love with you? Treasure your love for another in the same way. Don't let it turn into a dependent relationship. Offering unconditional love, love without demands, is the only way of evoking similar feelings in another. Let go of the desire to receive or commandeer. Give your love just for the sake of it, without expecting anything in return and then perhaps a miracle will happen and you will be loved in return.

Interpretation

Imagine yourself standing in front of the mirror of the world. If your image is one of love, then the reflection will be the same. If your image contains the desire for mutual affection, you can forget about seeing mutual love in the reflection. The mirror will simply reflect your vain attempts to be somebody else's favourite. When love turns into a dependent relationship, excess potential is created which brings about a kind of energetic 'pressure drop'. Dependent relationships are created by setting conditions along the lines of, «If you don't want to marry me you obviously do not love me. If you love me, you are good. If you don't love me you are bad.» The greater the desire to possess, i.e. to be loved back, the greater the effect of balancing forces which will do anything to spite you. Love, not tied to conditions, is free from possession, avoids dependent relationships and generates creative, positive energy. Only unconditional love is capable of working the miracle of mutual love.

71. Polar Comparisons

Principle

Constantly comparing yourself to others leads to an inferiority complex in the case that you undervalue your worth and a superiority complex if you overestimate your worth. Both are equally monstrous. Be aware that pendulums force you to compare yourself to certain standards because it is to their advantage that everyone walk abreast in a single formation. Turn your 'non-normality' into self-sufficiency. Claim the right not to be the same as everyone else. Smash the pendulum rule: «Be like me, and do as I do». Always observe the Transurfing rule instead: «Give yourself permission to be you and allow others to be different». When you do fall out of line, the pendulum will follow you as if you were the new normal.

Interpretation

Don't imagine that everyone else around you attributes as much significance to your shortcomings and strengths as you do. In reality, everyone is concerned with their own persona, so you can boldly shake this titanic burden from your shoulders. The artificial need to be 'fabulous' very often pushes people to copy others who have already achieved this title. Mindlessly copying someone else's script will create nothing more than a parody. Everyone has their own script. All you have to do is choose your personal credo and then walk your talk. In any group, the leaders are always the ones who live true to their own credo. They become leaders because they have freed themselves from the responsibility of consulting others on the matter of how they should behave. Leaders have no need to imitate anyone. They simply know their worth and know what to do. They don't try to curry favour and they have nothing to prove. When you come to know your own worth, everyone else around you will automatically do the same.

72. The Unique Soul

Principle

You are a truly unique individual. Your unique-ness is beyond competition. Claim the right to your originality and you will have a huge advantage over others who follow more well-trodden trends and paths. Trying to be like him (or her) never works. Be yourself. Indulge yourself that luxury. If you put on the mask of an existing star, you will only ever be a copy or a parody. No one ever became a star by copying someone else. You will succeed when you stop trying to be like other people; You will succeed when you stop repeating the experience of others; You will succeed when you acknowledge the splendour of your own individuality. Then others will have no choice but to concur.

Interpretation

The fact that you deserve the best and that you are capable of anything has been hidden from you very carefully. People will tell you that you are naive to believe that you have unlimited capabilities but in fact, the opposite is true. You are capable of creating a fabulous masterpiece, making ingenious discover-ies, achieving outstanding results in sports, business, and any other professional activity. All you have to do is turn to your heart. The heart has access to all knowledge, creation and achievement. The task is to allow yourself to be yourself. What have the masks you wear ever done to help you achieve success, abundance or happiness? There is no point in changing yourself. That would be just another mask. If you get rid of the masks imposed on you by destructive pendulums, the treasure hidden in your soul will be revealed. You truly deserve the best because you are a truly extraordinary, miraculous creation. Just allow yourself to be it.

73. The Miserly Mind

Principle

When a person's mind is in the pendulums' grip, they are forced to accept endless limitations and fulfil the role allocated to them in the game. Do not listen to the mind, which wants to convince you that your goal is unrealistic. Remember, the mind is locked in a framework of false stereotypes. Life will eventually end and your dream will remain lying alone in a dusty drawer. Without the heart, the mind is not capable of very much in this world. Together they are capable of anything because the union of heart and mind gives rise to a magical power, the power of outer intention. Don't give up on your dream simply because some pumped-up authority has claimed the right to decide what is realistic and what isn't. Claim the right to a personal miracle.

Interpretation

The mind treats the heart as if it were a child asking you to buy it a favourite toy in a toyshop. The responses of the mind are usually fairly standard, such as, «We can't afford it. Don't be silly! I know best what you need. That's not for the likes of us. That's unrealistic. Not everyone is so blessed. You don't have the skills or the abilities. He (she) is way out of your league! Just be like everyone else.»

The mind works according to logic, which is imposed by pendulums who benefit from keeping their followers on a short leash, denying them the freedom to choose their dreams. For the heart, there is no logic. It interprets everything literally. The mind says you have no money but the heart doesn't want money, it wants the toy! Motivated by the fact that you have no money, the mind places a ban on the toy (it's not realistic, its unachievable), and all the heart can do is retreat into itself and forget about it. With that, you've just witnessed the funeral of your personal dream. The mind cannot fathom how to make the dream come true and so it won't let the dream into the layer of your personal world because as far as the mind is concerned, everything in life has to be logical and clear. All you have to do is agree to have, and outer intention will take care of the 'how'.

74. The Greedy Soul

Principle

What makes a person one of the elite? The answer? Their own unique path. As soon as you go your own way, the treasures of the world will be revealed to you and then others will look at you and wonder how you do it. Have the audacity not to give a damn about stereotypes; Have the audacity to believe in the limitless possibilities of the soul; Have the audacity to claim the right to your own great personality. If the mind will allow it, the soul will find a way to realise your dream. Don't be too shy to go the whole hog and order anything you want. Be realistic, demand the impossible.

Interpretation

Whatever goal you set for yourself, it will be difficult to achieve within the context of a rational worldview. The stereotype of the unachievable goal is the most rigid of all. The mind will ask, «How do I achieve it?» That is when your heart needs to say, «Be quiet, that's not your concern. We are choosing a toy!» When you are at the threshold of making a choice, limitations should be of no concern to you whatsoever. Did you want to have a boat? What about having your own yacht? Did you want to have a flat? What about your own mansion? Did you want to be head of department? What about being president of the corporation? Did you want to buy a cheap plot of land and build your own house? What about having your own island in the Mediterranean? Did you want to work a lot to earn a lot of money? How about not working at all and living for your own pleasure? The list of 'what about's' could go on forever. You cannot imagine how modest your requests are in comparison to what you could have if you went after your own personal goal through your own personal door.

75. Money

Principle

Above all, start moving towards your goal and then money will follow on automatically, as an accompanying attribute. If you are not on your own true path yet, remember this rule: "Don't think about the fact that you don't have enough money. Think about having money." Concentrate on the fact that you have money. It doesn't matter how much. The important thing is that you have it and that soon you will have more of it. Receive money with love and joy and let go of it easily. Don't scrimp and save. The more you scrimp, the less you will have. Likewise, don't accumulate large sums of money without saving for something, in particular, otherwise, you will lose it. Create movement. Funds flow through a pipe, not through a reservoir.

Interpretation

When a 'have-not' stands at a shop counter, they count every penny wondering how to economise, spend as stingily as possible and constantly complaining about how expensive everything is. Their thoughts are focused on one thing: there is never enough money. This thought pattern is manifested in physical reality. How could it be otherwise? They are standing in front of a mirror. Don't think about the money you don't have. Think about the money you do have. You will always find something in your purse. If you don't have the funds for a certain purchase right now, do not spend time regretting it. Just put it off until later. You know that the funds will soon appear. This way you create the corresponding image, which will gradually become reflected in reality.

There is another powerful ritual you can use. Collect all the small, abandoned coins you can find, particularly the rusty ones that no one else bothers to pick up and place them carefully in a small box repeating the thought form: "You are home now, dear coins. I will look after you and you will call money to me. I take care of money and money loves me and comes to me." Try it and see.

76. Comfort Zone

Principle

People are free to choose whatever they want; it is just that not many believe that it is theirs to do so.

If you feel unsure of yourself when you are trying on wealth, fame and giddy success for size, it is clearly

143

still out of your comfort zone. If it isn't in your comfort zone, it will never be yours. However, you can expand the zone. Create a mental slide of your goal and hold it permanently in sight. Return to the mental picture you have drawn again and again. Relish the details, add new elements to the picture, and learn to see yourself in a different way. You deserve the very best. It is all realistic. There are no constraints. The limits are all in your mind.

Interpretation

Positive slides can help introduce the incredible into your comfort zone. When you stop feeling waves of uneasiness from the thought that your dream might be accessible to you, doubts will cease and belief will be transformed into knowledge. The heart will come into harmony with the mind and you will feel the resolve to have. It is pointless trying to persuade the heart; the heart does not discourse, it simply knows. The heart cannot be persuaded but it can be trained. It has to get used to the new comfort zone. Don't worry if you still feel unsure and don't see how your goal can be realised. Continue systematically visualising the slide. When the goal is completely integrated into your comfort zone, outer intention will open the door to the world of your dreams. This is a fortress taken by lengthy siege.

77. Allies

Principle

You are only alone to the extent that you desire to be alone. Any inanimate object can be transformed into an entity and made your ally if you treat it as if it were animate. You can create your own talisman, a toy of some kind, and with all seriousness, consider that it is alive and helping you. Everything around you, buildings, trees, furniture, dishes, home appliances, cars and computers will all help you and look after you if you decide that this is the case. Don't ask your allies for anything. Treat them in the same way that you treat the mirror of the world. Be confident that they are looking after you. Know this and regularly repeat the thought to yourself.

Interpretation

Just as the physical body can create like from like, so can the heart. When you think of an object as a living being, your thought form transforms into an energetic entity, a kind of phantom with a 'virtual soul'. Phantoms are invisible and intangible because they exist in a metaphysical space. Nonetheless, once born they exist objectively and are capable, like any thought form, of influencing physical reality. So, if you want to, you can boldly animate the objects around you and communicate with them as you would with living beings. Treat them with affection, respect, and love and

145

they will repay you in kind. For example, if you treat your car as if it were a living being you care about very much, its «soul» will guard you from accidents. When you have to throw something away, don't forget to thank it first. Don't worry, as soon as you forget about items that you no longer need, their 'virtual soul' will cease to exist.

78. Guardian Angel

Principle

If you are having a hard time and have no one to lean on, create yourself a guardian angel. If you believe in your guardian angel, they will exist and the opposite is also true. If you don't believe in your guardian angel, they won't exist. The very thought that there is a being who looks after you and you alone helps give you a balanced feeling of confidence. Never take offence at your angel, to say nothing of getting angry with them. You have no idea what misfortune your angel is doing its utmost to protect you from. Celebrate your successes but don't forget to thank your guardian angel and remind your angel that you love them. This will make your angel stronger and they will reward you handsomely.

Interpretation

Is it true that every person has their own guardian angel? That is for you to decide. You create your own reality. As long as you believe in angels, yours will exist as an energetic entity, and if you are convinced that your angel is looking after you, then that will be true. Pagans who worshipped all sorts of invented gods and fetishes were no fools. You can picture your guardian angel as taking any form. Of itself, it does not look like anything. You give it form with your imagination. So imagine your angel taking the guise you feel comfortable with. If you feel lonely, share your feelings with your angel. If you are dealing with some misfortune or even cause for joy, share this with your angel too. The more sincerely you love your angel and express your gratitude for all kinds of little things, the more powerful it will become and the more help it can give you. Remember, there is no such thing as a fantasy. Any invention of the mind is already a reality.

Made in the USA
Coppell, TX
24 April 2023